KU-245-577

Free
Voluntary
Reading

Stephen Krashen

LIBRARIES UNLIMITED

AN IMPRINT OF ABC-CLIO, LLC
Santa Barbara, California • Denver, Colorado • Oxford, England

Copyright 2011 by Stephen Krashen

All rights reserved. No part of this publication may be reproduced, stored in a retrieval system, or transmitted, in any form or by any means, electronic, mechanical, photocopying, recording, or otherwise, except for the inclusion of brief quotations in a review or reproducibles, which may be copied for classroom and educational programs only, without prior permission in writing from the publisher.

Library of Congress Cataloging-in-Publication Data

Krashen, Stephen D.
    Free voluntary reading / Stephen Krashen.
        p. cm.
    Includes bibliographical references and index.
    ISBN 978-1-59884-844-1 (pbk. : acid-free paper)—ISBN 978-1-59884-845-8 (ebook) 1. Silent reading—United States. 2. Language arts—United States. 3. Literacy—United States. 4. Children—Books and reading—United States. I. Title.
    LB1050.55.K73   2011
    418'.4—dc22   2011003414

ISBN: 978-1-59884-844-1
EISBN: 978-1-59884-845-8

15 14 13 12 11   1 2 3 4 5

This book is also available on the World Wide Web as an eBook.
Visit www.abc-clio.com for details.

Libraries Unlimited
An Imprint of ABC-CLIO, LLC

ABC-CLIO, LLC
130 Cremona Drive, P.O. Box 1911
Santa Barbara, California 93116-1911

This book is printed on acid-free paper ∞
Manufactured in the United States of America

014615840 Liverpool Univ

Free
Voluntary
Reading

Contents

Introduction

This book is an attempt to present the progress made in free voluntary reading over the last decade, since the completion of the second edition of *The Power of Reading*. It is all good news: Free voluntary reading looks better and more powerful than ever. And the alternatives to free reading as a means of developing high levels of literacy look weaker than ever.

Chapter one, "Eighty-Three Generalizations About Free Voluntary Reading," has undergone many revisions since I wrote the first version about five years ago. This is because so much updating has been necessary—new studies keep appearing with more evidence for the advantages of reading and in different areas. (Did you know some studies show that pleasure reading delays the onset of dementia?) I have no doubt that by the time this book is published, this chapter will once more be behind the times.

Nearly all the research covered in *The Power of Reading* is from studies of English readers, those reading in English as either a first or second language. Chapters two and three tell us that the power of reading applies to other languages (chapter two) and in different contexts (chapters two and three). This is supported by a wide range of studies using different methodologies. The conclusion: Free reading works everywhere and with everyone.

Next, some controversies: "Should We Reward Recreational Reading?" (chapter four) is the most recent in a series of papers I have written analyzing research that claims to support the use of Accelerated Reader, the most popular reading management program in North America. Once again, Accelerated Reader does not deliver: There still remains no evidence that it is worth the investment or even that it works at all.

Chapter five discusses the widely held belief that there has been a decline in literacy in the United States. Not so. Those claiming that there is a decline have made serious errors in presenting the data, as well as omissions. If this was deliberate, it suggests that those responsible are using strategy similar to the Shock Doctrine as described by Naomi Klein.

The public has the view that all children need to become good readers is a stiff dose of phonics. Again, not so. A modest amount of phonics instruction can indeed be helpful in making texts more comprehensible, but chapter six argues that "intensive systematic phonics" helps children do better only on tests in which they pronounce lists of words. This insight was initially provided by Prof. Elaine Garan in response to the National Reading Panel report, and I provide more evidence that Garan is right.

Chapters seven and eight attempt to expand our discussion. In chapter seven, I present evidence suggesting that surfing the Internet will help second language acquirers, and I suggest a path for those interested to try it themselves.

Chapter eight presents some hypotheses that I think deepen the concept of free voluntary reading. They claim that reading results in more literacy and language development when reading appears to be effortless, and we are so focused on the message that we don't notice that it contains language (grammar and vocabulary) that we have not yet acquired. For those reading in a second language, optimal acquisition happens when readers are not even aware that the text is in another language. This chapter also suggests that the more comprehension checking teachers require, the less development of literacy takes place. This is directly contrary to the current view that "focus on form" and explicit direct instruction is the path to literacy and language competence. It also concludes that "hard work" and suffering are indications that literacy development is not taking place. I am not claiming that everything that is fun is good for you, but for literacy development at least, the path of pleasure is the only one that works.

Eighty-Three Generalizations About Free Voluntary Reading

1

Earlier version published in *Children and Adolescents*, Published by Young Learners (Children and Adolescents) Special Interest Group of the International Association of Teachers of English as a Foreign Language. 1/2009, pages 7–12.

Summary: *I present here a set of generalizations about free voluntary reading. Most are supported by empirical evidence, but some are supported only in anecdotal reports. Those in this category are marked with an asterisk (*). All are invitations for additional research.*

The set of generalizations begins with research on free voluntary reading done in school, known as Sustained Silent Reading (SSR). In SSR, time is set aside for recreational reading. Students read whatever they like (within reason) and are not tested on what they read.

Research on Sustained Silent Reading

Language Development

1. Overall, SSR is successful: In 51 out of 54 comparisons, readers do as well as or better than comparison students in reading comprehension (Krashen 2001a). SSR students did better in every comparison in a review of studies (23 comparisons) of SSR among students of English as a foreign language (Krashen 2007).

2. Longer-term studies tend to be more successful (Krashen 2001a).

SSR students also do better than comparisons on tests of:

3. writing (studies reviewed in Krashen 2004a; Hsu and Lee 2007).

4. writing fluency (Mason 2007, but see K. Smith 2007).

5. spelling (in most cases; see Krashen 2004a).

6. vocabulary (Krashen 2004a).

7. grammar (Krashen 2004a; Rodrigo 2006; Mason 2007).

SSR is Robust

8. SSR works for languages other than English: Japanese (Hito-sugi and Day 2004), Spanish (Rodrigo, Krashen, and Gribbons 2004) as foreign language, see chapter 2 in this volume.

9. SSR works for both first and second language acquisition (Krashen 2004a).

10. SSR works for foreign language acquisition for children (Elley and Mangubhai 1983; Cho and Kim 2004; Cho and Kim 2005), college students (Mason and Krashen 1997; S. Y. Lee 2007; C. K. Liu 2007), high school (age 15–16) students (K. Smith 2006), evening college students (K. Smith 2007), and vocational college students (Hsu and Lee 2007).

11. SSR works for all ages of readers studied so far (Krashen 2004a).

12. SSR often works even if some conditions are not met (S. Y. Lee 2004, 2007).

13. SSR works with graded readers (Mason and Krashen 1997).

The most important question one can ask about any reading activity is whether it helps create a lifelong reader (Calkins 2004). Results from SSR are encouraging:

Establishing a Reading Habit

14.   SSR readers report that they read more at the end of the SSR program than at the beginning (Pilgreen and Krashen 1993).

15.   SSR readers report reading more several years after participating in an SSR program (Greaney and Clarke 1973).

Heritage Language

16.   Classes that emphasize popular literature and free reading promote heritage language development (McQuillan 1998a).

17.   Second generation speakers of Korean who speak their heritage language better report more free reading in Korean (Cho and Krashen 2000).

18.   Heritage language speakers who have developed high levels of competence in their heritage language, despite spending very little time in the country where the heritage language is spoken, all report having access to reading materials in the heritage language, and nearly all developed an interest in reading in the language for pleasure (Tse 1998).

What Is the Most Effective Is Also the Most Pleasant: Affect and SSR

19.   Foreign language, second language, and heritage students prefer SSR to regular instruction (McQuillan 1994; Dupuy 1997; Lao and Krashen 2008).

20.   A single SSR session can change attitudes (K. S. Cho and Krashen 2002).

21.   Teachers note fewer discipline problems when SSR is done (Petre 1961; Takase 2004).

Do They Read During SSR?

22.   Observations show that 90 percent of students read during SSR (Von Sprecken and Krashen 1998; Cohen 1999).

23.   More reading takes place if books are available in class and students do not have to bring their own reading material every time (Von Sprecken and Krashen 1998).

24.   More reading takes place if the teacher reads while students are reading (Von Sprecken and Krashen 1998; Wheldall and Entwhistle 1998).

25.   SSR may not work if it is done schoolwide at the same time each day (Minton 1980).

26.   SSR is not effective if done during the students' lunch period (Maynes 1981).

The Assumption Has Been Made That SSR Is "Not Enough": Can SSR Be Made Stronger?

27.   Supplementation with writing does not increase the power of reading (Mason 2004; K. Smith 2006).

28.   Supplementation with writing and error correction does not increase the power of reading (Mason 2004).

29.   Supplemental activities that make reading more comprehensible and interesting can increase the power of reading (Manning and Manning 1984).

Results of Correlational Research Are Consistent with the Results of SSR Studies

30.   Those who read more read better (Krashen 2004a).

31.   Those who read more write better (Krashen 2004a; S.Y. Lee 2004).

32.   Those who read more have better vocabularies (Lee, Krashen, and Tse 1997; Cho, Park, and Krashen 2008).

33.   Those who read more have more grammatical competence (Y. O. Lee, Krashen, and Gribbons 1996).

34.   Those who read more spell better (Polak and Krashen 1988).

35.   Those who read more read faster (Anderson, Wilson, and Fielding 1988).

36.   Those who read more know more about literature (Ravitch and Finn 1987; West, Stanovich, and Mitchell 1993).

37.   Those who read more know more about science and social studies (Stanovich and Cunningham 1993).

38.   Those who read more have more "cultural literacy" (West, Stanovich, and Mitchell 1983).

39.   Those who read more have more "practical knowledge" (Stanovich and Cunningham 1993).

40.   More Bible reading is related to more knowledge of the Bible, but more "study" of the Bible is not related to more knowledge of the Bible (Filback and Krashen 2002).

41.   Those who read more get better grades in writing class (S. Y. Lee and Krashen 2002).

42.   Those who read more do better on the TOEFL (Test of English as a Foreign Language) (Gradman and Hanania 1991; Constantino, S. Y. Lee, K. S. Cho, and Krashen 1997; see also Mason 2006).

43.   Those who read more have less writing apprehension (S. Y. Lee 2001; S. Y. Lee and Krashen 1996, 1997).

44.   Those who read more suffer less from writer's block (S. Y. Lee 2001, 2004).

Additional Benefits

45.   Older people who continue to read show less memory loss and suffer fewer effects of dementia (Rice 1986; Galluccia et al. 2009; Verghese et al. 2003).

46.   Reading causes relaxation and may help you fall asleep (Nell 1988).

47.   Free voluntary reading is a "flow" experience (Nell 1998; Massimini, Csikszentmihalyi, and Della Fave 1992).

48.   Nearly all eminent people were voracious readers: "[O]mnivorous reading in childhood and adolescence correlates positively with ultimate adult success" (Simonton 1988).

Encouraging Reading

49.   "Reluctant readers" are often those with little access to books (Worthy and McKool 1996).

50.   Those who have more access to books do more recreational reading (Krashen 2004a).

51.   Those who have more access to books read better (Krashen 2004a; McQuillan 1998b; Krashen, S. Y. Lee, and McQuillan 2010).

52.   More access to school libraries is related to more recreational reading (Houle and Montmarquette 1984; McQuillan and Au 2001).

53.   Children with access to better classroom libraries read more (Morrow and Weinstein 1982).

54.   Better access to public libraries results in more recreational reading (Ramos and Krashen 1998; Lao 2003).

55.   Children get many of their books for recreational reading from libraries (Krashen 2004a).

56.   Children who live in low-income neighborhoods have very little access to books (Smith, Constantino, and Krashen 1996; Neuman and Celano 2001).

57.   Children who live in low-income neighborhoods have fewer books at home (Feitelson and Goldstein 1986).

58.   Children who live in low-income neighborhoods have less access to books at school (Smith, Constantino, and Krashen 1996; Duke 2000).

59.   Classroom and school libraries don't always have what children like to read. Children from high-income families can find these books elsewhere, but children of poverty cannot (Worthy, Moorman, and Turner 1999).

60.   Bookstores with children's and adolescent literature are far more plentiful in high-income neighborhoods (Neuman and Celano 2001).

61.   Access to books is as strong a factor in school success as poverty. This holds for both school libraries (Achterman 2008; Krashen, S. Y. Lee, and McQuillan 2010) and books in the home (Schubert and Becker, 2010; Evans, Kelley, Sikora, and Treieman 2010).

62.   Students of English as a foreign language often have little access to recreational reading in English (H. K. Kim and Krashen 1997).

63.   Read-alouds (reading to children) encourage children to read more (Brassell 2003; Martinez et al. 2007; Wang and Lee 2007; K. S. Cho and D. S. Choi 2008).

64.   When compelling and comprehensible reading material is available, direct encouragement can result in children reading more (Shin 2003).

65.   Children read more when they have a quiet and comfortable place to read (Morrow 1983; Greaney and Hegarty 1987).

66.   There is no scientific evidence showing that providing children with rewards increases reading development (McQuillan 1997; Krashen 2003, 2005a).

67.   There is no evidence that the use of lexiles or similar means of determining reading difficulty encourages more reading (Krashen 2001b).

68.   Middle school boys who read more comics report more reading in general, more book reading, and interest in reading (Ujiie and Krashen 1996).

69.   Case histories show that comics can serve as a conduit to "heavier" reading (Krashen 2004a).

70.   One positive experience (one "home run book") can create a reader (Trelease 2006; Von Sprecken, J. Kim, and Krashen 2000; J. Kim and Krashen 2000; Ujiie and Krashen 2002).

71.   Home run book experiences vary widely among children (Ujiie and Krashen 2002).

72.   Home run books are not necessarily "quality" books (Ujiie and Krashen 2002).

73.   Prize-winning books are not particularly popular among children (Ujiie and Krashen 2006).

74.   Peers influence reading (Appleby and Conner 1985; Wendelin and Zinck 1983; Worthy 1998).

75.   Book displays influence reading (Morrow 1982).

76.   TV watching, unless excessive, is not a threat to recreational reading (Neuman 1995).

77.   Those who regularly use computers do not spend less time reading (Gallup 2002). In fact, more time spent on the computer is modestly related to more recreational reading for adults (Robinson and Godbey 1997) and adolescents (de Haan and Huysmans 2004).

78. More use of the Internet among adolescents in low-income families results in more reading (Jackson et al. 2006).

79. Contrary to popular opinion, there is no solid evidence of a decline in reading in the United States (Krashen 2004b).

80. Contrary to popular opinion, children do not lose all interest in reading as they get older (Krashen and Von Sprecken 2002; Schatz and Krashen 2006).

81. Reading interests among young readers broaden as they get older (LaBrant 1958).

82. Good readers tend to be "narrow readers" (Lamme 1976).

83. "Narrow reading" can stimulate more recreational reading (Cho and Krashen 1994, 1995a, 1995b).

Guidelines for SSR

The following suggestions are based on the generalizations presented above as well as on the suggestions of teachers.

1. Do a little each day, not a lot once a week (distributed, not massed).

2. Less is more; do less than you think they can handle. If you think students can sit and read for 15 minutes, do 10 minutes.

3. Make sure plenty of books and other reading material are available.

4. Comic books are okay.

5. Magazines are okay.

6. Graded readers, books written for language students, are okay.

7. Let students select their own reading material (S. Y. Lee 2007).

8. Impose minimum censorship on what is read* (for discussion, see Trelease 2004).

9. It is okay for readers to read "easy" books (below their "level") (Krashen 2005b).

10. It is okay for readers to read "hard" books (above their "level") (Krashen 2005b).

11. Students don't have to finish every book they start to read.

12. Sustained silent reading is not for beginners. Beginners need other kinds of comprehensible text. It also will not help advanced readers who have already established a reading habit (Krashen 2001a).

13. Supplement SSR with activities that serve to make reading more comprehensible and interesting (e.g., read-alouds, trips to the library, discussion of literature).

14. Don't use rewards for reading, don't test students on what is read, and don't require book reports. Use zero or minimum accountability. When the conditions are right (compelling reading material available, and enough reading competence), direct encouragement can work.

15. How about some food and drink? Let's trying eating and reading in the school library (Trelease and Krashen 1996).

References

Achterman, D. 2008. "Haves, Halves, and Have-Nots: School Libraries and Student Achievement in California." PhD diss., University of North Texas. http://digital.library.unt.edu/permalink/meta-dc-9800:1.

Anderson, R., P. Wilson, and L. Fielding. 1988. Growth in reading and how children spend their time outside of school. *Reading Research Quarterly* 23: 285–303.

Appleby, B., and J. Conner. 1965. Well, what did you think of it? *English Journal* 54: 606–12.

Brassell, D. 2003. Sixteen books went home tonight: Fifteen were introduced by the teacher. *The California Reader* 36(3): 33–39.

Calkins, H. 2004. Letter to the editor. *Education Week*, September 29, 2004.

Cho, G., and S. Krashen. 2000. The role of voluntary factors in heritage language development: How speakers can develop the heritage language on their own. *ITL: Review of Applied Linguistics*, 127–128: 127–140.

Cho, K. S., and S. Krashen. 1994. Acquisition of vocabulary from the Sweet Valley High Kids series: Adult ESL acquisition. *Journal of Reading* 37: 662–67.

Cho, K. S., and S. Krashen. 1995a. From Sweet Valley Kids to Harlequins in one year. *California English* 1(1): 18–19.

Cho, K. S., and S. Krashen. 1995b. Becoming a dragon: Progress in English as a second language through narrow free voluntary reading. *California Reader* 29: 9–10.

Cho, K. S., and S. Krashen. 2002. Sustained silent reading experiences among Korean teachers of English as a foreign language: The effect of a single exposure to interesting, comprehensible reading. *Reading Improvement* 38(4): 170–74.

Cho, K. S., and D. S. Choi. 2008. Are read-alouds and free reading "natural partners"? *Knowledge Quest* 36(5): 69–73.

Cho, K. S., E. J. Park, and S. Krashen. 2008. Reading in English by children in Korea: Frequency, effectiveness and barriers. *Indonesian JELT*, 4(1): 18–25.

Cho, K. S., and Hee-Jung Kim. 2005. Using the newspaper in an English as a foreign language class. *Knowledge Quest* 34(4): 47–49.

Cho, K. S., and Hey-Jung Kim. 2004. Recreational reading in English as a foreign language in Korea: Positive effects of a sixteen-week program. *Knowledge Quest* 32(4): March/April 2004.

Cohen, K. 1999. Reluctant eighth grade readers enjoy sustained silent reading. *California Reader* 33(1): 22–25.

Constantino, R., S. Y. Lee, K. S. Cho, and S. Krashen. 1997. Free voluntary reading as a predictor of TOEFL scores. *Applied Language Learning* 8: 111–18.

de Haan, J., and F. Huysmans. 2004. IT/Media use and psychological development among Dutch youth. *IT&Society* 1(7): 44–58.

Duke, N. 2000. For the rich it's richer: Print experiences and environments offered to children in very low- and very high-socioeconomic status first-grade classrooms. *American Educational Research Journal* 37(2): 441–78.

Dupuy, B. 1997. Voices from the classroom: Students favor extensive reading over grammar instruction and practice, and give their reasons. *Applied Language Learning* 8(2): 253–61.

Elley, W., and F. Mangubhai. 1983. The impact of reading on second language learning. *Reading Research Quarterly* 19: 53–67.

Evans, M., J. Kelley, J. Sikora, and D. Treiman. 2010 Family scholarly culture and educational success: Books and schooling in 27 nations. *Research in Social Stratification and Mobility*, in press.

Feitelson, D., and Z. Goldstein. 1986. Patterns of book ownership and reading to young children in Israeli school-oriented and nonschool-oriented families. *Reading Teacher* 39(9): 924–30.

Filback, R., and S. Krashen. 2002. The impact of reading the Bible and studying the Bible on biblical knowledge. *Knowledge Quest* 31(2): 50–51.

Galluccia, M., P. Antuono, F. Ongaro, P. Forloni, D. Albani, G. Amicia, and C. Reginia. 2009. Physical activity, socialization and reading in the elderly over the age of seventy: What is the relation with cognitive decline? Evidence from "The Treviso Longeva (TRELONG) study." *Archives of Gerontology and Geriatrics* 48(3): 284–86.

Gallup. 2002. Does reading still stack up? Gallup Poll News Service, September 3, 2002. http://www.gallup.com.

Gradman, H., and E. Hanania. 1991. Language learning background factors and ESL proficiency. *Modern Language Journal* 75: 39–51.

Greaney, V., and M. Clarke. 1973. A longitudinal study of the effects of two reading methods on leisure-time reading habits. In *Reading: What of the future?* ed. D. Moyle. London: United Kingdom Reading Association, pp. 107–14.

Greaney, V., and M. Hegarty. 1987. Correlations of leisure time reading. *Journal of Research in Reading* 10: 3–20.

Hitosugi, C. I., and R. Day. 2004. Extensive reading in Japanese. *Reading in a Foreign Language* Volume 16, No. 1.

Houle, R., and C. Montmarquette. 1984. An empirical analysis of loans by school libraries. *Alberta Journal of Educational Research* 30: 104–14.

Hsu, Y. Y., and S. Y. Lee. 2007. A three-year longitudinal study of in-class sustained silent reading with Taiwanese vocational college students. *Selected papers from the Sixteenth International Symposium on English Teaching, English Teachers' Association—Republic of China.* Taipei: Crane Publishing Company.

Jackson, L., A. von Eye, F. Biocca, G. Barbatsis, Y. Zhao, and H. Fitzgerald. 2006. Does home Internet use influence the academic performance of low-income children? *Developmental Psychology* 42(3): 429–33.

Johnson, R. 1965. Individualized and basal primary reading programs. *Elementary English* (42): 902–904, 915.

Kim, H. K., and S. Krashen. 1997. Why don't language acquirers take advantage of the power of reading? *TESOL Journal* 6,3: 26–29. Reprinted in *The Adult Education Reader*, Winter 1997, 3(4): 26–33.

Kim, J., and S. Krashen. 2000. Another home run. *California English* 6(2): 25.

Krashen, S. 2001a. More smoke and mirrors: A critique of the National Reading Panel report on fluency. *Phi Delta Kappan* 83: 119–23.

Krashen, S. 2001b. The lexile framework: Unnecessary and potentially harmful. *CSLA (California School Library Association) Journal* 24(2): 25–26.

Krashen, S. 2003. The (lack of) experimental evidence supporting the use of Accelerated Reader. *Journal of Children's Literature* 29(2): 9, 16–30.

Krashen, S. 2004a. *The power of reading*. Portsmouth, NH: Heinemann Publishing Companies, and Westport, CT: Libraries Unlimited.

Krashen, S. 2004b. Letter to the editor. *The School Library Journal* 50(11): 13.

Krashen, S. 2005a. Accelerated Reader: Evidence still lacking. *Knowledge Quest* 33(3): 48–49.

Krashen, S. 2005b. Is in-school free reading good for children? Why the National Reading Panel report is (still) wrong. *Phi Delta Kappan* 86(6): 444–47.

Krashen, S. 2007. Extensive reading in English as a foreign language by adolescents and young adults: A meta-analysis. *International Journal of Foreign Language Teaching* 3(2): 23–29.

Krashen, S., and D. Von Sprecken. 2002. Is there a decline in the reading romance? *Knowledge Quest* 30(3): 11–17.

Krashen, S., S. Y. Lee, and J. McQuillan. 2010. An analysis of the PIRLS (2006) data: Can the school library reduce the effect of poverty on reading achievement? *CSLA Journal*, in press. California School Library Association.

LaBrant, L. 1958. An evaluation of free reading. In *Research in the three R's*, ed. C. Hunnicutt and W. Iverson. New York: Harper and Brothers, pp. 154–61.

Lamme, L. 1976. Are reading habits and abilities related? *Reading Teacher* 30: 21–27.

Lao, C. Y. 2003. Prospective teachers' journey to becoming readers. *New Mexico Journal of Reading* 32(2): 14–20.

Lao, C. Y., and S. Krashen. 2008. Do students like what is good for them? An investigation of the pleasure hypothesis with middle school students of Mandarin. *International Journal of Foreign Language Teaching* 4(2): 19–20.

Lee, S. Y. 2001. *What makes it difficult to write*. Taipei: Crane Publishing Company.

Lee, S. Y. 2004. The robustness of extensive reading: Evidence from two studies. Presentation at English Teachers Association Conference, Taipei, and Jalt, Osaka.

Lee, S. Y. 2007. Revelations from three consecutive studies on extensive reading. *RELC Journal* 38 no. 2, 150–70.

Lee, S. Y., and S. Krashen. 1996. Free voluntary reading and writing competence in Taiwanese high school students. *Perceptual and Motor Skills* 83: 687–90.

Lee, S. Y., and S. Krashen. 1997. Writing apprehension in Chinese as a first language. ITL: Review of Applied Linguistics 115–116: 27–37.

Lee, S. Y., and S. Krashen. 2002. Predictors of success in writing in English as a foreign language: reading, revision behavior, apprehension, and writing. *The College Student Journal* 36(4): 532–43.

Lee, S. Y., S. Krashen, and L. Tse. 1997. The author recognition test and vocabulary knowledge: A replication. *Perceptual and Motor Skills* 83: 648–50.

Lee, Y. O., S. Krashen, and B. Gribbons. 1996. The effect of reading on the acquisition of English relative clauses. *ITL: Review of Applied Linguistics*, 113–114: 263–273.

Liu, C. K. 2007. A reading program that keeps winning. *Selected papers from the Sixteenth International Symposium on English Teaching, English Teachers' Association—Republic of China*. Taipei: Crane Publishing Company.

Manning, G., and M. Manning. 1984. What models of recreational reading make a difference? *Reading World* 23: 375–80.

Martinez, M., N. Roser, J. Worthy, S. Strecker, and P. Gough. 1997. Classroom libraries and children's book selections: Redefining "access" in self-selected reading. In *Inquires in literacy: Theory and practice. Forty-sixth yearbook of The National Reading Conference*, ed. C. Kinzer, K. Hinchman, and D. Leu. Chicago: National Reading Conference, pp. 265–72.

Mason, B. 2004. The effect of adding supplementary writing to an extensive reading program. *International Journal of Foreign Language Teaching* 1(1): 2–16.

Mason, B. 2006. Free voluntary reading and autonomy in second language acquisition: Improving TOEFL scores from reading alone. *International Journal of Foreign Language Teaching* 2(1), 2–5.

Mason, B. 2007. The efficiency of self-selected reading and hearing stories on adult second language acquisition. *Selected papers from the Sixteenth International Symposium on English Teaching, English Teachers' Association—Republic of China*. Taipei: Crane Publishing Company.

Mason, B., and S. Krashen. 1997. Extensive reading in English as a foreign language. *System* 25: 91–102.

Massimini, F., M. Csikszentmihalyi, and A. Della Fave. 1992. Flow and biocultural evolution. In *Optimal experience: Psychological studies of flow in consciousness*, ed. M. Csikszentmihalyi and I. Csikszentmihalyi. Cambridge: Cambridge University Press, pp. 60–81.

Maynes, F. 1981. Uninterrupted sustained silent reading. *Reading Research Quarterly* 17: 159–60.

McQuillan, J. 1994. Reading versus grammar: What students think is pleasurable for language acquisition. *Applied Language Learning* 5: 95–100.

McQuillan, J. 1997. The effects of incentives on reading. *Reading Research and Instruction* 36: 111–25.

McQuillan, J. 1998a. The use of self-selected and free voluntary reading in heritage language programs: A review of research. In *Heritage language development*, ed. S. Krashen, L. Tse, and J. McQuillan. Culver City: Language Education Associates, pp. 73–87.

McQuillan, J. 1998b. *The literacy crisis: False claims and real solutions*. Portsmouth, NH: Heinemann Publishing Company.

McQuillan, J., and J. Au. 2001. The effect of print access on reading frequency. *Reading Psychology* 22: 225–48.

Minton, M. 1980. The effect of sustained silent reading upon comprehension and attitudes among ninth graders. *Journal of Reading* 23: 498–502.

Morrow, L. 1982. Relationships between literature programs, library corner designs, and children's use of literature. *Journal of Educational Research* 75: 339–344.

Morrow, L. 1983. Home and school correlates of early interest in literature. *Journal of Educational Research* 75: 339–44.

Morrow, L., and C. Weinstein. 1982. Increasing children's use of literature through program and physical changes. *Elementary School Journal* 83: 131–37.

Nell, V. 1988. *Lost in a book*. New Haven: Yale University Press.

Neuman, S. 1995. *Literacy in the television age: The myth of the TV effect*. 2nd ed. Norwood, NJ: Ablex.

Neuman, S., and D. Celano. 2001. Access to print in low-income and middle-income communities. *Reading Research Quarterly* 36(1): 8–26.

Petre, B. 1983. Reading breaks make it in Maryland. *The Reading Teacher* 15: 191–194.

Pilgreen, J., and S. Krashen. 1993. Sustained silent reading with English as a second language high school students: Impact on reading comprehension, reading frequency, and reading enjoyment. *School Library Media Quarterly* 22: 21–23.

Polak, J., and S. Krashen. 1988. Do we need to teach spelling? The relationship between spelling and voluntary reading among community college ESL students. *TESOL Quarterly* 22: 141–46.

Ramos, F., and S. Krashen. 1998. The impact of one trip to the public library: Making books available may be the best incentive for reading. *The Reading Teacher* 51(7): 614–15.

Ravitch, D., and C. Finn. 1987. *What do our 17-year-olds know?* New York: Harper and Row.

Rice, E. 1986. The everyday activities of adults: Implications for prose recall—Part I. *Educational Gerontology* 12: 173–86.

Robinson, J., and G. Godbey. 1997. *Time for life: The surprising way Americans use their time.* University Park, PA: University of Pennsylvania Press.

Rodrigo, V. 2006. The amount of input matters: Incidental acquisition of grammar through listening and reading. *International Journal of Language Teaching* 2(1): 10–13.

Rodrigo, V., S. Krashen, and B. Gribbons. 2004. The effectiveness of two comprehensible-input approaches to foreign language instruction at the intermediate level. *System* 32(1): 53–60.

Schatz, A., and Krashen, S. 2006. Attitudes toward reading in grades 1-6: Some decline in enthusiasm but most enjoy reading. *Knowledge Quest* 35: 46–48.

Schubert, F., and Becker, R. 2010. Social inequality of reading literacy: A longitudinal analysis with cross-sectional data of PIRLS 2001 and PISA 2000 utilizing the pair wise matching procedure. *Research in Social Stratification and Mobility* 29: 109–133.

Shin, F. 2003. Should we just tell them to read? The role of direct encouragement in promoting recreational reading. *Knowledge Quest* 32(3).

Simonton, D. 1988. *Scientific genius: A psychology of science.* Cambridge: Harvard University Press.

Smith, C., R. Constantino, and S. Krashen. 1996. Differences in print environment for children in Beverly Hills, Compton and Watts. *Emergency Librarian* 24(4): 4–5.

Smith, K. 2006. A comparison of "pure" extensive reading with intensive reading and extensive reading with supplementary activities. *International Journal of Foreign Language Teaching* 2(2): 12–15.

Smith, K. 2007. The effect of adding SSR to regular instruction. *Selected papers from the Sixteenth International Symposium on English Teaching, English Teachers' Association—Republic of China.* Taipei: Crane Publishing Company.

Stanovich, K., and A. Cunningham. 1993. Where does knowledge come from? Specific associations between print exposure and information acquisition. *Journal of Educational Psychology* 85(2): 211–29.

Takase, A. 2004. Japanese high school students' motivation to read extensively. Presented at the JALT conference, Nara, Japan, November 2004.

Takase, A. 2004. Censorship and children's books. Trelease-on-reading .com/censor_entry.html.

Trelease, J. 2006. *The Read-aloud handbook.* 6th ed. New York: Penguin.

Trelease, J., and S. Krashen. 1996. Eating and reading in the school library. *Emergency Librarian* 23(2): 27.

Tse, L. 1998. Ethnic identity formation and its implications for heritage language development. In *Heritage language development*, ed. S. Krashen, L. Tse, and J. McQuillan. Culver City: Language Education Associates, pp. 15–29.

Ujiie, J., and S. Krashen. 1996. Is comic book reading harmful? Comic book reading, school achievement, and pleasure reading among seventh graders. *California School Library Association Journal* 19(2): 27–28.

Ujiie, J., and S. Krashen. 2002. Home run books and reading enjoyment. *Knowledge Quest* 31(1): 36–37.

Ujiie, J., and S. Krashen. 2006. Are prize-winning books popular among children? An analysis of public library circulation. *Knowledge Quest* 34(3): 33–35.

Verghese, J., R. Lipton, M. Katz, C. Hall, C. Derby, G. Kuslansky, A. Armbrose, M. Silwinski, and H. Buschke. 2003. Leisure activities and the risk of dementia in the elderly. *New England Journal of Medicine* 348: 2508–16.

Von Sprecken, D., and S. Krashen. 1998. Do students read during sustained silent reading? *California Reader* 32(1): 11–13.

Von Sprecken, D., J. Kim, and S. Krashen. 2000. The home run book: Can one positive reading experience create a reader? *California School Library Journal* 23(2): 8–9.

Wang, F. Y., and S. Y. Lee. 2007. Storytelling is the bridge. *International Journal of Foreign Language Teaching* 3(2): 30–35.

Wendelin, K., and R. Zinck. 1983. How students make book choices. *Reading Horizons* 23: 84–88.

West, R., K. Stanovich, and H. Mitchell. 1993. Reading in the real world and its correlates. *Reading Research Quarterly* 28: 35–50.

Wheldall, K., and J. Entwhistle. 1988. Back in the USSR: The effect of teacher modeling of silent reading on pupils' reading behaviour in the primary school classroom. *Educational Psychology* 8, 51–56.

Worthy, J. 1998. "On every page someone gets killed!" Book conversations you don't hear in school. *Journal of Adolescent and Adult Literacy* 41(7): 508–17.

Worthy, J., and S. McKool. 1996. Students who say they hate to read: The importance of opportunity, choice, and access. In *Literacies for the 21st century: Research and practice*, ed. D. Leu, C. Kinzer, and K. Hinchman. Chicago: National Reading Conference. 245–56.

Worthy, J., M. Moorman, and M. Turner. 1999. What Johnny likes to read is hard to find in school. *Reading Research Quarterly* 34(10): 12–27.

Does the Power of Reading Apply to All Languages?

2

Originally published in *Language Magazine*,
vol 9 (9), 2010, pp. 24–27.

Summary: *The power of reading is well established. For English.*

The evidence is overwhelming that reading for pleasure—that is, self-selected recreational reading—is the major source of our ability to read, to write with an acceptable writing style, to develop vocabulary and spelling abilities, and to handle complex grammatical constructions. The evidence holds both for English as a first language and for English as a second and foreign language.

Three kinds of studies show that more English reading results in higher levels of English literacy:

1.   Correlational: These studies show that those who read more, or say they read more, develop higher levels of literacy. The usual problem with this kind of research is that "correlation is not causation"; that is, some other factor may be responsible for both more reading and more literacy development. But many of these studies control for potential "confounds" using multivariate statistical methods, and thus clearly suggest that reading is indeed the real cause of the greater literacy development.

2.   Case studies: A number of studies have been published describing those who have attained high levels of literacy, and reading is given the credit. Even though these case histories are not "scientific" experiments, quite often pleasure reading is the only possible explanation for the high level of literacy attained. We have yet to see case studies of those with high levels of literacy who were not readers.

3.   Experimental: Experimental studies are the most convincing. In these studies, groups of students are compared who experience the same treatment in school, with one exception: One group does self-selected reading for a period of time in their language arts or English as a Second Language or English as a Foreign Language class.

The details for English are presented in other publications (e.g., Krashen 2004; chapter 3 of this volume).

What about other languages? I attempt here to see if the power of reading holds for

1.   first language development in children,

2.   "heritage" languages, that is, languages spoken by the children of immigrants or those who immigrated to a country when young, and

3.   second/foreign languages.

The details are below, but the results are very easy to state: The power of reading clearly extends to languages other than English.

First Language Development

More reading results in more literacy development

Correlational studies

Verhoeven and Aarts (1988): Verhoeven and Arts found a positive (but low) correlation between the amount of reading done in Turkish and tests of literacy for sixth-grade Turkish-speaking children living in the Netherlands and in Turkey. The low correlation may have been due to little reading being done by either group: Both were low SES (low socioeconomic status; in other words, high poverty), which means little reading material was available at school or at home.

Shu, Anderson, and Zhang (1995): Third- and fifth-grade students in Beijing, China, who reported more reading outside of school did better on a vocabulary test of "difficult words" (words thought to be unfamiliar to the children). (See table 13, page 89.)

Lee (1996): Lee reported positive but modest correlations between the amount of pleasure reading Taiwanese high school students said they did in Mandarin and their performance on a standardized writing test (see also Lee and Krashen 1996).

Rodríguez-Trujillo (1996): When a library was introduced into a school in Venezuela, children read more. Those sixth graders who read the most made the greatest gains on a test of reading comprehension and vocabulary.

Heritage Language

More reading results in more literacy development

Correlational studies

Cho and Krashen (2000): Second generation heritage language speakers of Korean who reported greater proficiency in Korean reported more pleasure reading in Korean (and also more TV watching, greater parental use, and more trips to Korea when young; all these factors were independent predictors of reported heritage language proficiency).

Case studies

Tse (2001): Ten heritage language speakers (of Spanish, Cantonese, and Japanese) developed high levels of proficiency in English and the heritage language despite having done little or no study in the country where the language is spoken. All had "literacy experience in the heritage language in the home and community at an early age" (p. 691). "The most frequently mentioned activity the participants engaged in independently was reading for pleasure" (p. 692). Pleasure reading choices included comic books, popular magazines, and nonfiction. We cannot conclude that pleasure reading was the only reason for the high level of heritage language competence; Tse notes that all ten had a peer group and parents that supported use of the heritage language, and attended schools that valued the heritage language.

Experimental studies

McQuillan (1996): University-level students of Spanish for native speakers took a ten-week course that included self-selected reading and literature circles based on popular literature. Readers made better gains in vocabulary than comparisons and reported improvement in reading ability in Spanish.

Schon, Hopkins, and Davis (1982): Low SES second, third, and fourth graders did self-selected reading in Spanish for 60 minutes per week for eight months from high interest books. The third and fourth graders did better than comparisons on vocabulary and reading tests, while second graders did better on vocabulary and were equivalent to comparisons in reading.

Schon, Hopkins, and Vojir (1984): Tempe Study: High school students in Tempe, Arizona, were asked to do sustained silent reading in their heritage language (Spanish) for 12 minutes per day for four months. There was no difference in reading comprehension between the readers and comparisons, but students could choose to read in English.

Schon, Hopkins, and Vojir (1984): The Chandler Study: High school students did SSR in Spanish for seven months. There was no difference between readers and comparisons in reading comprehension, but not all teachers carried out the treatment faithfully, and some comparison group students did pleasure reading in Spanish. (Note: As McQuillan [1997] points out, in both of these studies there was much less interest in reading in Spanish among U.S.-born students than among more recently arrived immigrants.)

Schon, Hopkins, and Vojir (1985): Seventh and eighth graders read popular reading material in Spanish for 45 minutes a week for eight and a half months. Readers did better than comparisons on reading speed and vocabulary, but only in classes in which teachers carried out the treatment faithfully.

Foreign Language Studies

More reading results in more literacy development

Correlational studies

Stokes, J., S. Krashen, and J. Kartchner (1998): For students of Spanish as a foreign language at the university level, acquisition of the subjunctive was related to the amount of free voluntary reading done in Spanish, not to amount of study, including specific study of the subjunctive, or length of residence in a Spanish-speaking country.

Case studies

Leung (2002): Self-selected reading in Japanese by a sophisticated adult acquirer for 20 weeks resulted in perceived gains in reading ability and documented gains in vocabulary.

Arnold (2009): Advanced students of German as a foreign language did self-selected reading (seven sessions of 75 minutes each) from the Internet. Students reported improvement in reading ability and vocabulary.

Grabe and Stoller (1997): A beginning adult acquirer of Portuguese with an extensive background in linguistics improved in reading and vocabulary with self-selected reading over five months. This reader reported that he was a dedicated dictionary user.

Pigada and Schmidt (2006): An adult acquirer of French (low-intermediate) did one month of extensive reading of simplified readers (about one book per week) with no other exposure to French. Improvement in spelling and vocabulary knowledge was documented.

Experimental studies

Day and Hitosugi (2004): Second semester university students of Japanese read children's books in Japanese for ten weeks, and did better than traditional students on a traditional test of reading comprehension in Japanese, and just as well on other measures.

Rodrigo, Krashen, and Gribbons (2004): Fourth semester students of Spanish as a foreign language at the university level did an extensive reading class that combined self-selected and assigned reading, and made better gains than a traditional group in vocabulary and grammar, with no difference on a cloze test.

Discussion

The survey confirms that self-selected reading works. On a theoretical level, this conclusion supports the Comprehension Hypothesis, the claim that we acquire language by understanding it (Krashen 2003). The obvious practical implication is that if we are serious about encouraging literacy development, we need to be serious about providing access to reading materials.

Clearly, this is not happening. Governments are spending huge amounts, in the name of literacy, on developing standards and on enforcing the standards through testing, but paying, at best, only lip service to improving libraries.

The frequent rationale for not funding libraries is the complaint that "giving them books won't help; they won't read anyway." There are two responses to this complaint:

The first is that if there are no books, it is certain that no reading will take place.

The second is that the "they won't read" accusation is wrong. It is incorrect for English reading and for reading in other languages. Given access to books, young people read.

High school students in Taiwan who live in more "print-rich" environments report doing more pleasure reading (Lee 1996). Rodríguez-Trujillo (1996) reported that sixth graders in Venezuela attending schools with school libraries reported more voluntary reading than children in similar schools without a school library. These results are identical to those already reported for English (Krashen 2004).

Also, as is the case for the English language (Krashen 2004), access to quality school libraries is associated with better reading development. Students with access to the library in Rodríguez-Trujillo (1996) did better on tests of Spanish vocabulary and reading comprehension. Krashen, Lee, and McQuillan (2010) reported that more access to school libraries of at least 500 books was associated with higher reading scores for 10-year-olds in 40 countries, tested in their own language. This result held even when SES was controlled, and is similar to results reported by Elley (1996) based on tests administered by the IEA (The International Association for the Evaluation of Educational Achievement) given to 9- and 14-year-olds in 32 countries.

We must invest in libraries.

References

Arnold, N. 2009. Online extensive reading for advanced foreign language learners: An evaluation study. *Foreign Language Annals* 42(2): 340–66.

Cho, G., and S. Krashen. 2000. The role of voluntary factors in heritage language development: How speakers can develop the heritage language on their own. *ITL: Review of Applied Linguistics* 127–128: 127–40.

Day, R., and C. Hitosugi. 2004. Extensive reading in Japanese. *Reading in a Foreign Language* 16(1): 20–38.

Elley, W. 1996. Lifting literacy levels in developing countries: Some implications from an IEA study. In *Promoting reading in developing countries*, ed. V. Greaney. Newark, DE: International Reading Association, pp: 39–54.

Grabe, W., and F. L. Stoller (1997). Reading and vocabulary development in a second language: A case study. In *Second language vocabulary acquisition*, ed. J. Coady and T. Huckin. Cambridge: Cambridge University Press, pp. 98–122.

Krashen, S. 2003. *Explorations in language acquisition and use: The Tapei lectures*. Portsmouth, NH: Heinemann Publishing Company.

Krashen, S. 2004. *The power of reading*. Portsmouth, NH: Heinemann, and Westport, CT: Libraries Unlimited.

Krashen, S., S. Y. Lee, and J. McQuillan (in press). An analysis of the PIRLS (2006) data: Can the school library reduce the effect of poverty on reading achievement? *CSLA Journal* (California School Library Association).

Lee, S. Y. 1996. The relationship of free voluntary reading to writing proficiency and academic achievement among Taiwanese senior high school students. *Proceedings of the Fifth International Symposium on Language Teaching*. Taipei: Crain, pp. 119–26.

Lee, S. Y., and S. Krashen. 1996. Free voluntary reading and writing competence in Taiwanese high school students. *Perceptual and Motor Skills* 83: 687–90.

Leung, C. Y. 2002. Extensive reading and language learning: A diary study of a beginning learner of Japanese. *Reading in a Foreign Language* 14(1): 66–81.

McQuillan, J. 1996. How should heritage languages be taught? The effects of a free voluntary reading program. *Foreign Language Annals* 29, 56–72.

McQuillan, J. 1997. The use of self-selected and free voluntary reading in heritage language programs: A review of research. In *Heritage language development*, ed. S. Krashen, L. Tse, and J. McQuillan. Culver City: Language Education Associates. pp. 73–87.

Pigada, M., and N. Schmidt. 2006. Vocabulary acquisition from extensive reading: A case study. *Reading in a Foreign Language*, 18(1): 1–28.

Rodrigo, V., S. Krashen, and B. Gribbons. 2004. The effectiveness of two comprehensible-input approaches to foreign language instruction at the intermediate level. *System* 32(1): 53–60.

Rodríguez-Trujillo, N. 1996. Promoting independent reading: Venezu-elan and Columbian experience. In *Promoting reading in developing countries*, ed. V. Greaney. Newark, DE: International Reading Association, pp: 109–29.

Schon, I., K. Hopkins, and W. Davis. 1982. The effects of books in Spanish and free reading time on Hispanic students' reading abilities and attitudes. *NABE Journal* 7: 13–20.

Schon, I., K. Hopkins, and C. Vojir. 1984. The effects of Spanish reading emphasis on the English and Spanish reading abilities and attitudes of Hispanic high school students. *The Bilingual Review* 11: 33–39.

Schon, I., K. Hopkins, and C. Vojir. 1985. The effects of special reading time in Spanish on the reading ability and attitudes of Hispanic junior high school students. *Journal of Psycholinguistic Research* 14: 57–65.

Shu, H., R. C. Anderson, and H. Zhang. 1995. Incidental learning of word meanings while reading: A Chinese and American cross-cultural study. *Reading Research Quarterly* 30: 76–95.

Stokes, J., S. Krashen, and J. Kartchner. 1998. Factors in the acquisition of the present subjunctive in Spanish: The role of reading and study. *ITL: Review of Applied Linguistics* 121–122: 19–25.

Tse, L. 2001. Resisting and reversing language shift: Heritage language resilience among U.S. native biliterates. *Harvard Educational Review* 71(4): 676–706.

Verhoeven, L., and R. Aarts. 1998. Attaining functional biliteracy in the Netherlands. In *Literacy development in a multilingual context*, ed. A. Durgunoglu and L. Verhoeven. Mahwah, NJ: Erlbaum, pp: 111–33.

Extensive Reading in English as a Foreign Language by Adolescents and Young Adults: A Meta-Analysis

3

Originally published in *International Journal of Foreign Language Teaching* 3(2): 23–29.

Abstract: *A review of studies of extensive reading adolescents and young adults studying English as a foreign language revealed a strong and consistent positive effect for both tests of reading comprehension (mean effect size = .88 for nine studies) and cloze tests (mean = .73, 14 studies). Students provided with more access to reading (titles per student) did significantly better on tests of reading comprehension, but there was no relationship between access and performance on cloze tests.*

Despite the consistently positive results of extensive reading programs, there still seem to be doubts as to their effectiveness: Study after study says they work, but very few language programs have adopted them. This paper takes another look at the research, focusing on studies of extensive reading using adolescent and adult students of English as a foreign language.[1] Older students of English as a foreign language (EFL) students are an appropriate group to study for both practical and theoretical reasons. Mastery of English is, of course, crucial for nearly all activities that involve any kind of international communication. Also, focusing on foreign language removes one potential confound, the easy availability of English outside the classroom.

There are two goals of this meta-analysis. The first is to determine whether free reading has an overall positive effect. The second goal is to determine the factors that contribute to the overall effect.

We will be able to accomplish the first goal and take some steps toward reaching the second goal.

The studies examined here were all published in professional journals or conference proceedings. Studies were done in Taiwan (Yuan and Nash 1992; Sims 1996; Sheu 2005; Hsu and Lee 2005, 2007; Lee 2005a, 2006; K. Smith 2006, 2007; Liu 2007), the Philippines (Lituanas, Jacobs, and Ranayda 1999), Japan (Mason and Krashen 1997), and Yemen (Bell 2001).

In all studies, time was set aside for self-selected reading. Studies in which a significant percentage of reading was assigned are not included here (e.g., Lee 2005b; Lao and Krashen 2000), and only studies that included reading tests (see below) are included.

Two kinds of reading tests were considered, cloze tests and tests of reading comprehension. The impact of extensive reading was determined by computing effect sizes. The usual formula for the effect size is the mean of the experimental group minus the mean of the comparison group, all divided by the pooled standard deviation, based on posttest scores. This formula was used here, and when possible the effect of the pretest was taken into consideration by subtracting the effect size of the pretest from that of the posttest. The mean effect size for all studies is a measure of the overall impact of extensive reading.

Data on two factors that could influence the impact of extensive reading was included in the analysis: access to reading material and duration of treatment.

Access

For first language development, access to reading material has been consistently shown to be a predictor of how much students read and how well they read (Krashen 2004). In this analysis, book access was represented by total titles available to students and the number of book titles per student.

Duration

Previous reviews have shown that longer SSR programs tend to be more effective than shorter programs (Krashen 2001). Duration is included here in terms of the number of weeks, months, or academic years the program lasted. This is a crude measure because it does not consider the amount of time set aside for reading each day or week.

A number of other factors are undoubtedly relevant to predicting the impact of extensive reading programs, but their inclusion will await additional studies, when methods are developed for representing their contributions quantitatively.

Results

Table 1 presents data on access, duration of the program, and the results of cloze tests and reading comprehension tests.

Overall, extensive reading programs clearly produce positive effect sizes. All 13 effect sizes for cloze tests and all nine effect sizes for reading comprehension were positive.

For unknown reasons, sample size was negatively correlated with measures, with studies with fewer subjects producing larger effect sizes (for cloze tests, $r = -.45$, $p = .11$; for reading comprehension, $r = -.81$, $p < .011$). For this reason, weighted means were calculated, resulting in adjusted means of .73 for cloze tests and .88 for reading comprehension.

Table 1
Mean titles per student and effect sizes

	mean	sd	n
titles/S	17.5	32.1	18
cloze	0.79 (.73)	0.46	13
RC	1.06 (.88)	0.87	9

n = number of studies
( ) = adjusted for sample size

Details of the studies, as well as notes on effect size calculations, are presented in table 2. In some cases, effect sizes were calculated for each experimental group in a given publication. This was not possible in other cases. Thus, the average values calculated here should be considered approximate. For studies with no results listed, it was either not possible to calculate effect sizes from the data provided or cloze tests or reading comprehension were not used as measures.

In Liu (2007), sample size and titles per student were calculated on the basis of students and titles per class. More than one class was involved in these studies. The Liu (2007) effect size is an average calculated from five experimental classes and 12 comparison classes over four years.

For Yuan and Nash (1992), the effect size in table 2 is the average of three methods of calculating the score (from the t-score of gains, comparison of mean gain scores, pre- and posttests).

The reading comprehension test used in K. Smith (2006) also included usage and listening, and was given five months after the course ended.

In Sims (1996), two different experimental classes were used. The number of titles was estimated from the total number of books: 700 books were provided, and "most" were separate titles (Sims, personal communication).

Table 2
Access, duration, and effect sizes

study	n	titles	titles/S	duration	ES Cloze	ES RC
Yuan & Nash 1992	37	200	5.4	one year	0.38	
Sims 1996	30	550	18.3	one year		0.81
Sims, 1996	30	550	18.3	one year		0.65
Mason retakers	30	100	3.3	one sem	0.702	
Mason Jr college	31	200	6.4	one year	1.47	
Mason university	40	200	5	one year	1.11	
Mason: response L1	40	550	13.75	one year	0.24	0.61
Mason: response L2	36	550	15.28	one year	0.63	0.48
Lituanas et al. 2001	30			6 months		1.7
Bell 2001	14	2000	142.9	one year	1.31	3.14
Sheu 2003	31	57	1.84			0.71
Sheu 2003	34	55	1.62			1.04
Lee 2005a	65	215	3.3	12 weeks	0.24	
Hsu & Lee 2005	47	354	7.5	one year	0.58	
K. Smith 2006	51	500	9.8	one year	0.47	0.39
Lee 2006	41	1200	29.3	one year	1.02	
Hsu & Lee 2007	47	500	10.6	3 years		
K. Smith 2007	41	500	12.2	one year	0.56	
Liu 2007	46	450	9.8	one year	1.59	

Effect size = Cohen's d.

All effect sizes take pretests into account (ES posttest – ES pretest) for reading comprehension, except for Mason (Mason and Krashen, 1997), which was based only on the posttest.

n = number of students in extensive reading group

titles/S = number of separate book titles per student

All Mason studies from Mason and Krashen (1997)

Mason: response L1 = students wrote summaries in Japanese; response L2 = students wrote summaries in English

Number of titles in Mason, response in L1, response in L2 from Mason (personal communication)

Inspection of table 1 shows that there was little variability in duration in the studies in this sample. Most studies lasted for one academic year. Thus, duration was not examined as a predictor of effect sizes.

The relationship between total titles and titles per student was strong ($r = .91$). Thus, only titles per student was used in the analysis.

Titles per student was modestly correlated with cloze test effect sizes, and the correlation was close to statistical significance ($r = .35$, n= 13, p = .12, one-tail). Because of the influence of sample size, a multiple regression was done with sample size and titles/students as predictors (table 3). The relationship between access and reading comprehension was not significant in this analysis.

Table 3
Predictors of effect sizes for cloze tests (13 studies):
Multiple regression

predictor	b	se	t	p
n	−0.016	0.014	1.13	0.142
titles/S	0.0009	0.0045	0.208	0.42

Adjusted r2 = .067
n = sample size
titles/S = titles per student

Eight studies provided data for both reading comprehension and titles per student. In contrast to the cloze test results, the two were nearly perfectly correlated ($r = .95$). Because of the influence of sample size on scores of reading comprehension, the impact of titles per student on reading comprehension scores was investigated using multiple regression, controlling for sample size. As presented in table 4, number of titles per student was a highly significant predictor.

Table 4
Predictors of effect sizes for reading comprehension (8 studies)

predictor	b	se	t	p
n	−0.021	0.015	1.42	0.11
titles/S	0.015	0.0033	4.51	0.003

Adjusted r2 = .91

n = sample size

titles/S = titles per student

According to these results, there is a strong impact of access: Setting the predicted number of students to the mean of the eight studies in table 2 (n = 33.3), and doubling the number of titles per student (from 27 to 88) would increase the effect size for reading more than a third of a standard deviation (from .98 to 1.36).

Summary and Discussion

The clearest result of this study is that extensive reading is consistently effective. The average effect size for both measures was over .70. There were no negative effect sizes; the smallest effect size was .24.

The attempt to study factors contributing to successful extensive reading results has clearly only just begun. Data from eight studies using tests of reading comprehension showed that providing more titles per student had a substantial effect on the outcome of the study, but this relationship was not present for tests of reading comprehension.

It is surprising that even this much of a relationship between access and the effect of extensive reading was found, because so many other factors are probably at work.

First, access defined as titles per student, as noted above, is a crude measure. A modest number of books, if they are the right ones, can have a strong impact, and supplying large quantities of books will not help if the books are not interesting and comprehensible.

Also, as noted earlier, other factors undoubtedly play a role. These include:

1. The duration of the program (Krashen 2001).

2. The length of time and frequency of each reading session, i.e., massed versus distributed sessions.

3. The extent of comprehension checking: Krashen (2007) has hypothesized that more frequent and more detailed comprehension checking will result in less interest in reading and less progress in literacy development. (See also chapter 8, this volume.)

4. Whether reading is encouraged by the use of read-alouds, conferencing, and discussion, all of which have empirical support (Krashen 2004).

5. Whether students are under pressure because of heavy academic loads and exams. Those in SSR programs do more pleasure reading on their own outside of class (Sims 1996), and it is likely that this contributes to the success of the program. Pressure from exams and other courses can reduce the amount of time students devote to reading. According to student reports, this was the case in Hsu and Lee (2007).

Conclusion

This review provides more evidence that in-school self-selected reading works. It must be emphasized that effect sizes were uniformly positive and typically quite impressive. In-school self-selected reading is effective and its effects are robust.

Note

1. There are, at the moment, not enough studies to warrant a meta-analytic review of extensive reading studies done with children acquiring

a second language. All studies using children that we have seen, however, have produced impressive evidence for "the power of reading" (Aranha 1985; Elley 1991; Elley and Mangubhai 1983; Cho and H. Y. Kim 2004; Cho and H. Kim 2005), with the exception of Williams (2007).

References

Aranha, M. 1985. Sustained silent reading goes East. *Reading Teacher* 39(2): 14–217.

Bell, T. 2001. Extensive reading: Speed and comprehension. The Reading Matrix 1(1). http://www.readingmatrix.com/articles/bell/index.html.

Cho, K. S., and Hee-Jung Kim. 2004. Recreational reading in English as a foreign language in Korea: Positive effects of a 16-week program. *Knowledge Quest* 32(4): 36–38.

Cho, K. S., and Hee-Jung Kim. 2005. Using the newspaper in an English as a foreign language class. *Knowledge Quest* 34(4): 47–49.

Elley, W. 1991. Acquiring literacy in a second language: The effects of book-based programs. *Language Learning* 41: 375–411.

Elley, W., and F. Mangubhai. 1983. The impact of reading on second language learning. *Reading Research Quarterly* 19: 53–67.

Hsu, Y. Y., and S. Y. Lee. 2005. Does extensive reading also benefit junior college students in vocabulary acquisition and reading ability? *The Proceedings of the 22nd International Conference in English Teaching and Learning*. Taipei: Crane Publishing Company, pp. 116–27.

Hsu, Y. Y., and S. Y. Lee. 2007. A three-year longitudinal study of in-class sustained silent reading with Taiwanese vocational college students. In *Selected Papers from the Sixteenth International Symposium on English Teaching, English Teachers' Association—Republic of China*. Taipei: Crane Publishing Company.

Krashen, S. 2001. More smoke and mirrors: A critique of the National Reading Panel report on fluency. *Phi Delta Kappan* 83: 119–23.

Krashen, S. 2004. *The power of reading*. Portsmouth, NH: Heinemann, and Westport, CT: Libraries Unlimited.

Krashen, S. 2007. Free reading in school: Three hypotheses. Paper presented at CELC conference, Singapore, May 2007.

Lao, C. Y., and S. Krashen. 2000. The impact of popular literature study on literacy development in EFL: More evidence for the power of reading. *System* 28: 261–70.

Lee, S. Y. 2005a. The robustness of extensive reading: Evidence from two studies. *International Journal of Foreign Language Teaching* 1(3): 13–19.

Lee, S. Y. 2005b. Sustained silent reading using assigned reading: Is comprehensible input enough? *International Journal of Foreign Language Teaching* 1(4): 10–12.

Lee, S. Y. 2006. A one-year study of SSR: University level EFL students in Taiwan. *International Journal of Foreign Language Teaching* 2(1): 6–8.

Lituanas, P. M., G. M. Jacobs, and W. A. Renandya. 1999. A study of extensive reading with remedial reading students. In *Language instructional issues in Asian classrooms*, ed. Y. M. Cheah and S. M. Ng. Newark, DE: International Development in Asia Committee, International Reading Association, pp. 89–104.

Liu, C. K. 2007. A reading program that keeps winning. In *Selected Papers from the Sixteenth International Symposium on English Teaching, English Teachers' Association—Republic of China*. Taipei: Crane Publishing Company.

Mason, B., and S. Krashen. 1997. Extensive reading in English as a foreign language. *System* 25: 91–102.

Sheu, S. P-H. 2004. Extensive reading with EFL learners at beginning level. *TESL Reporter* 36(2): 8–26.

Sims, J. 1996. A new perspective: Extensive reading for pleasure. *The Proceedings of the Fifth International Symposium on English Teaching*. Taipei: Crane Publishing Company, pp. 137–44.

Smith, K. 2006. A comparison of "pure" extensive reading with intensive reading and extensive reading with supplementary activities. *International Journal of Foreign Language Teaching (IJFLT)* 2(2): 12–15.

Smith, K. 2007. The effect of adding SSR to regular instruction. In *Selected Papers from the Sixteenth International Symposium on English Teaching, English Teachers' Association—Republic of China*. Taipei: Crane Publishing Company.

Williams, E. 2007. Extensive reading in Malawi: Inadequate implementation or inappropriate innovation? *Journal of Research in Reading* 30(1): 59–79.

Yuan, Y. P., and T. Nash. 1992. Reading subskills and quantity reading. *Selected Papers from The Eighth Conference on English Teaching and Learning in the Republic of China*. Taipei: Crane, pp. 291–304.

Should We Reward Recreational Reading?

4

Originally published in *Selected Papers from the Sixteenth International Symposium on English Teaching, English Teachers' Association, Republic of China*. Taipei: Crane Publishing Company, 2007, pp. 615–19.

Summary: *Evidence continues to mount supporting the practice of free voluntary reading. If free reading is beneficial, how can we encourage students to read more? A popular answer is to give children rewards for reading, and the most popular way of doing this in the United States is to use a commercial program, Accelerated Reader (AR). AR gives students points for passing tests on the content of the books they read, and the points can be exchanged for prizes. Although AR claims its research supports it, my surveys of the research show that AR has not been properly tested. In addition, there is reason to suspect that rewarding behavior that is intrinsically pleasant can extinguish the behavior because it sends the message that the activity is not pleasant and that people need to be bribed to do it.*

The language education profession knows a lot about encouraging reading. Among other things, increasing access to books helps, seeing other people read helps, reading aloud to students helps, and, of course, providing time for reading, as in sustained silent reading, helps (Krashen 2004). Trelease (2006) has suggested that one very positive reading experience can result in an interest in reading, a suggestion that has been confirmed in several studies (Von Sprecken, Kim, and Krashen 2000; Kim and Krashen 2000; Ujiie and Krashen 2002).

Instead of taking advantage of these inexpensive, well-supported, and reasonable options, many schools have turned to one that is very expensive and not well supported: rewarding children for reading, using "reading management" programs.

The most widely used of these programs is Accelerated Reader, now in use in 62,000 schools in North America (Renaissance Learning, press release 2007). There are signs of interest in the spread of AR to EFL worldwide.

Accelerated Reader (henceforth AR) consists of four components: (1) it provides lots of books; (2) it allots lots of time to read (AR recommends one hour per day, far more than is done in sustained silent reading); (3) it includes tests based on low-level facts contained in the book the child reads (for an example, see http://www.mrwrightsclass.com/ar/story.htm); (4) it awards prizes based on the number of points scored on the tests.

Evaluating Accelerated Reader

Renaissance Learning has claimed that numerous studies show AR increases reading ability in children who speak English as a first language. I have reviewed the research on AR in several papers (e.g., Krashen 2003, 2005) and concluded that AR has not yet been properly evaluated.

As noted above, AR has four elements:

1. lots of books

2. lots of time to read

3. tests

4. prizes

It has already been well established that (1) and (2), books and time to read, will result in substantial gains in reading (Krashen 2004). What we do not know is whether (3), tests, and (4), rewards, add anything.

Thus, a proper study should compare children in a full AR program, with elements (1)–(4), and children who receive only (1) and (2). Children in the "comparison group" should be given access to a large supply of books and plenty of time to read them. Unfortunately, this comparison has not been done: Studies compare AR with business-as-usual, "traditional" language arts programs. We thus have no idea whether elements (3) and (4), the tests and prizes, add anything.

Here is an analogy: I have just invented a new drug called KALM. It consists of sugar and Zoloft (a well-known antidepressant). It is expensive, costing significantly more than Zoloft alone. I have given it to a number of people, and they say they feel a lot better. Can I claim to have created a useful new product? Obviously not. It was the Zoloft that had the effect, not the sugar. People would save money by just taking Zoloft. Moreover, there may be long-term harm in adding sugar to the diet.

If it contains elements (1) and (2), AR should work, and quite often it does. That is, AR students do better in reading than comparisons with less access to books and less time to read, which is what we would expect. But, as I have noted in my reviews, there have been failures, cases in which AR students did no better than comparisons who, most likely, did not have as much access to books or as much time set aside to read.

A Recent Case

A recent example of this is Ross, Nunnery, and Goldfeder (2004). Ross et al. did two similar studies of children in grades 3, 4, and 5, comparing children who had a version of AR without rewards to comparison children. The results of both studies were nearly identical: Differences were small or nonexistent and not statistically significant. Table 1 presents effect sizes, which indicate the strength of a treatment. A positive effect size, in this case, means that the AR group did better. A negative effect size means the comparisons did better. Study 2 was republished as Nunnery, Ross, and McDonald (2006). (Ross et al. also includes a study of children in grades K, 1, 2, and 3; see Krashen 2007a for discussion of this sub-study.)

Table 1
Effect sizes: Ross et al.

Grade	Study 1	Study 2
3	0.33	0.36
4	−0.01	0.16
5	0.11	0.09
6	0.14	0.09

Cohen (1988) has recommended the following guidelines for the interpretation of effect sizes: An effect size of .2 is considered small, .6 is moderate, and .8 or more is considered large. The authors of the study (Nunnery et al., 2006) are somewhat more generous, considering a .36 effect size to be "strong" and .16 to be "small to moderate," but they agree that .09 is "no effect." On its Web site (www.renlearn.com), AR's parent company, Renaissance Learning, is even more enthusiastic about the impact of AR: .16 is now "moderate," and .09 is "small" (table 2). Most readers of the Renaissance Learning Web site, unfortunately, are probably not aware of the differences in interpretation.

Table 2
Interpretation of effect sizes in study 2

Grade	Effect size	Renlearn	Authors	Cohen
3	0.36	"large"	"strong"	between small and moderate
4	0.16	"moderate"	"small to moderate"	less than small
5, 6	.09, .09	"small, positive"	"no effect"	less than small

Cohen's benchmarks: .2 = small; .5 = medium; .8 = large

Authors' quotes from Nunnery et al. 2006

As is the case in other studies of AR, we must ask what AR was compared to. Comparisons had "sustained silent reading," but we are not told how much. We are also told that a "commercially available basal reading program" (Ross et al. 2006, p. 7) was used and that students participated in "small- and whole-group activities" (p. 7). It is thus doubtful that comparisons put in anywhere near as much time reading as the experimental group did: SSR is usually 10 to 20 minutes per day. Ross et al. report that 80 percent of AR teachers said they devoted at least 45 minutes per day to reading, and 95 percent said reading time was at least 30 minutes.

Is Accelerated Reader Harmful?

The results of this study and the results of others in which AR was no better than comparisons suggest that AR can be harmful: The AR students had more time to read, but did not do better. How can this be so? I suspect it is because of the tests.

It is possible that the use of AR tests emphasizing low-level, literal facts focused students on retaining small details of the books they read in order to achieve higher scores on tests. This means shallower involvement in reading and a smaller chance of entering the "Reading Zone" (Atwell 2007), the state of mind that readers are in when they are absorbed in a text. This state may be optimal for language acquisition and literacy development (Krashen 2007b). A shorter time reading, but spent in the Reading Zone, may be more effective than more reading outside the Zone.

There is another very serious problem. Kohn (1999) notes that "reading management" programs such as AR provide a reward for an activity that is already enjoyable, an extrinsic reward for something that is intrinsically pleasurable. When we do this, we run the danger of sending the message that the activity is not enjoyable, that nobody would do it without being bribed. A substantial amount of evidence shows that by giving children rewards inappropriately, we can "turn play into work" (Kohn 1999).

A Jump-Start?

It has been suggested that programs such as AR can "jump-start" reading, that the pleasure of reading will replace rewards once children discover how interesting books are. So far, there is no evidence that this takes place, no evidence that reluctant readers become dedicated readers because of incentives.

As part of a larger study, Robbins and Thompson (1991) examined the progress of seven low-achieving readers who participated in their reading incentive program. For at least four of the seven low achievers, the incentive program had no lasting effect. One low achiever, Walter, continued reading after the program ended (p. 67), but Timmy "didn't do much reading . . . once the summer reading program ended" (p. 65). Octavious earned all his points in the first few weeks, then his reading "slowed considerably" (p. 71). Sann "found little time for reading and library visits . . . as the summer ended" (p. 73). The incentive program clearly had no impact on Jason, who remained a reluctant reader (p. 69). Robbins and Thompson's analysis thus suggests that rewards do not "jump-start" reading interest (see also McQuillan 1997 for additional studies).

The Cost

At the time of this writing, AR software, without books, costs a school $4 U.S. per student per year, in addition to a one-time fee of $1,499. The average school library in the United States spends about $12 per year on books (calculated from 2004–5 data in Schontz and Farmer 2007). Many schools in the United States, in other words, are spending the equivalent of one-third of their book budget on software that has not produced any concrete evidence that it helps children.

Alternatives

Why even consider spending this kind of money without first trying more obvious means of encouraging reading? Wang and Lee (2007) easily and naturally combined several well-supported approaches into one to encourage reading among children in EFL classes in Taiwan, devoting a great deal of time to read-alouds for several years, which stimulated interest in books—especially series books such as Marvin Redpost—that the students read eagerly during sustained silent reading. The simple formula was:

Read-alouds/series books > home run book > time and place to read books of interest > free reading habit

Approaches like this one make much more sense.

References

Atwell, N. 2007. *The reading zone*. New York: Scholastic.

Cohen, J. 1988. *Statistical power for the behavioral sciences*. 2nd ed. Hillsdale, NJ: Erlbaum.

Kim, J., and S. Krashen. 2000. Another home run. *California English* 6(2): 25.

Kohn, A. 1999. *Punished by rewards: The trouble with gold stars, incentive plans, A's, praise, and other bribes*. 2nd ed. Boston: Houghton Mifflin.

Krashen, S. 2003. The (lack of) experimental evidence supporting the use of Accelerated Reader. *Journal of Children's Literature* 29(2): 9, 16–30.

Krashen, S. 2004. *The power of reading*. Westport, CT: Libraries Unlimited, and Portsmouth, NH: Heinemann.

Krashen, S. 2005. Accelerated Reader: Evidence still lacking. *Knowledge Quest* 33(3): 48–49.

Krashen, S. 2007a. Accelerated Reader: Once again, evidence still lacking. *Knowledge Quest* 36(1).

Krashen, S. 2007b. Hypotheses about free voluntary reading. In *The Proceedings of 2007 International Conference and Workshop on TEFL &*

Applied Linguistics, Department of Applied English, Ming Chuan University, Taiwan, ed. J. Myers and J. Linzmeier. Taipei: Crane Publishing Company, pp. 656–58.

McQuillan, J. 1997. The effects of incentives on reading. *Reading Research and Instruction* 36: 111–125.

Nunnery, J., S. Ross, and A. McDonald 2006. A randomized experimental evaluation of the impact of Accelerated Reader/Reading Renaissance implementation on reading achievement in grades 3 to 6. *Journal of Education for Students Placed at Risk* 11(1): 1–18.

Renaissance Learning 2007. Press release, July 18, 2007.

Robbins, E., and L. Thompson. 1991. A study of the Indianapolis-Marion County public library's summer reading program for children. ERIC Document ED 355 647.

Ross, S., J. Nunnery, and E. Goldfeder. 2004. *A randomized experiment on the effects of Accelerated Reader/Reading Renaissance in an urban school district: Preliminary evaluation report.* Memphis: The University of Memphis, Center for Research in Educational Policy.

Schontz, M., and L. Farmer. 2007. The SLJ spending survey. *School Library Journal* 53(1): 44–51.

Trelease, J. 2006. *The read-aloud handbook.* 6th ed. New York: Penguin.

Ujiie, J., and S. Krashen. 2002. Home run books and reading enjoyment. *Knowledge Quest,* 31(1): 36–37.

Von Sprecken, D., J. Kim, and S. Krashen. 2000. The home run book: Can one positive reading experience create a reader? *California School Library Journal* 23(2): 8–9.

Wang, F. Y., and S. Y. Lee. 2007. Storytelling is the bridge. *International Journal of Foreign Language Teaching* 3(2): 30–35.

The "Decline" in Reading in America: Another Case of the "Shock Doctrine"?

5

Originally published in *Substance*, **January 2008, p. 4, 6.**

Summary: *Has there been a decline in reading in the United States? Are Americans reading less and reading worse? A close look at the data shows that this is not so, which leads to the suspicion that reports of declines in reading are simply an example of the Shock Doctrine, a manufactured crisis designed to allow policies that would normally be unacceptable.*

The recent report from the National Endowment for the Arts (NEA), *To Read or Not To Read*, announced that Americans are reading less and reading worse. This resulted in a flurry of articles and reports in the media declaring that we were in a genuine state of crisis—e.g., there is a "remarkable decline" in reading (National Public Radio, November 19, 2007), "the young turn backs on books" (Dallas Morning News, November 20), and "the death of reading" (National Center for Policy Analysis, November 21). The head of the NEA, in fact, has stated that the "decline" in reading is the most important problem facing American society today.

There is indeed a crisis in reading. Few people, it seems, have read the NEA report, and the authors of the report did not do their reading homework. A close examination of the report reveals very little cause for concern. In fact, some of the data suggests that things are just fine.

Are Americans Reading Less?

17-Year-Olds

The argument that American youngsters are reading less comes from the NEA's table 18, in which young people of different ages (9, 13, and 17) were asked how often they read "for fun" in the years 1984, 1999, and 2004. The 9-year-olds show no change at all since 1984. The 13-year-olds show some decline (70 percent said they read "almost every day" or "once or twice a week" in 1984, but only 64 percent did so in 2004), and the 17-year-olds appear to have declined even more (64 percent in 1984 and 52 percent in 2004 said they read almost every day or once or twice a week). Also, the older the group, the less reading seems to be taking place.

One issue is how the youngsters interpreted the question: Responders sometimes don't think some kinds of reading are worth reporting. In one poll of teenagers, of 66 respondents who said they did "no reading," 49 checked several categories of leisure reading when asked what they liked to read (Mellon, *School Library Journal*, 1987).

This is a very likely factor when considering differences between older and younger readers and changes over time. The NEA cited a study by Kaiser (the M Generation study) in which young people were asked how much reading they did "yesterday." The NEA reports the results for book reading in the main text of its report: 63 percent of 8- to 10-year-olds, 44 percent of 11- to 14-year-olds, and only 34 percent of 15- to 18-year-olds read for at least five minutes "yesterday." It looks like those lazy 17-year-olds lose again. But in a footnote, the NEA mentions that if we include magazine and newspaper reading, there is no difference among the groups. I read the actual Kaiser report, and added the data on time spent looking at Web sites on the Internet to the data on book reading, magazine reading, and newspaper reading. If we total all reading, the 17-year-olds read the most, 60 minutes, and the other groups read quite a lot as well (the 8- to 10-year-olds read for 51 minutes, while the 11- to 15-year-olds read for 57 minutes).

Since 1984 there has, of course, been increased use of the Internet, as well as other forms of reading (e.g., graphic novels), and other forms of input of literate texts (audiobooks). We need to know if these kinds of reading were considered worth mentioning by respondents in 1999 and 2004 before we conclude that young people are reading less today.

College Students

The NEA presents data showing that college students read less than they did in high school. Not mentioned, however, is one study showing that college students read quite a bit, and this has not changed over three decades. Hendel and Harrold (*College Student Journal*, 2004) surveyed the leisure activities reported by undergraduates attending an urban university from 1971 to 2001. Among the questions asked were those related to leisure reading. In agreement with other studies, Hendel and Harrold reported a decline in newspaper reading and reading news magazines, but there was no decline in reported book reading. On a scale of 1–3 (1 = never, 2 = occasionally, 3 = frequently), the mean for book reading in 1971 was 2.35; in 2001 it was 2.26, with only small fluctuations in the years between 1971 and 2001.

Moreover, the ranking for reading books was higher than that reported for attending parties (2.14 in 2001), going to the movies (2.16), and for all categories of watching TV (sports = 2.07). Book reading held its own despite a clear enthusiasm for surfing the Internet (2.78) and e-mail (2.84), both newcomers.

Adults

To Read or Not To Read also tells us that 38 percent of adults said they read something yesterday, citing a 2006 Pew report. But they do not mention that according to a previous Pew study published in 2002, 34 percent said they read something yesterday. In 1991, this figure was 31 percent (see "Public's news habits little changed by September 11." Pew Research Center 2002). Also, a major study of reading published in 1945 found that only 21 percent of those ages 15 and older said they read something yesterday, with the most reading done by those lazy teenagers, ages 15–19: 34 percent (Link and Hopf, *People and Books*, 1945).

Are We Reading Worse?

The NEA used what many consider to be the gold standard for reading: The National Assessment for Educational Progress (NAEP) results, a national test given to samples of fourth, eighth, and 12th graders every few years. Once again, the problem is those lazy 17-year-olds, the 12th graders.

There are two kinds of NAEP tests: the long-term trends assessment, which allows comparisons of performance years apart, and main assessments, given every two years.

For the long-term trend scores, there has been no decline for fourth or eighth graders, but 12th graders scored four points less in 2004 than 12th graders did in 1984, which the NEA called a "downward trend."

There are several problems with concluding that this represents anything real. First, whether or not there has or has not been a decline depends on what year you use for the initial comparison: The 2004 national reading scores for 12th graders in 2004 are identical to those made by 12th graders in 1971. This is mentioned only in passing by the NEA. Here are the scores:

NAEP reading scores for 12th graders

1971: 285

1975: 286

1980: 285

1984: 289

1988: 290

1990: 290

1992: 290

1994: 288

1996: 288

1999: 288

2004: 285

Second, the "downward trend" since 1984 is quite small, four points on a test in which the highest 10 percent and lowest 10 percent differ by nearly 100 points. The NEA's chart 5B makes the "decline" look a lot larger than it is, charting only the changes, not the total scores, and using a y-axis ranging from –6 to +10. If the y-axis had included the entire range of scores, the differences would look quite small, which they are. Viewed in terms of the possible range in scores, NAEP results for 12th graders are remarkably consistent over the years.

The most outrageous misreporting in the NEA report is in their table 5F, where we are told that on main NAEP reading assessments, test scores for the lowest scoring 10 percent of 12th graders dropped 14 points between 1992 and 2005. A look at the actual NAEP report (The Nation's Report Card: 12th Grade Reading and Mathematics, 2005, page 2, figure 5) reveals that most of this happened between 1992 and 1994, a ten-point drop. Similarly, seven points of the nine-point drop between 1992 and 2004 for the lowest 25 percent occurred between 1992 and 1994. Clearly, something was wrong with one of those tests.

It is hard to see how anyone can look at the figure in the NAEP report and conclude that the drop occurred between 1992 and 2004. A look at the figure also shows that this one-time unusual drop is the only real change in NAEP scores since 1992.

In other words, much of the fuss about declines in reading scores is really about scores for a subgroup of 12th graders between 1992 and 1994. It is not clear whether the authors of the NEA report deliberately constructed table 5F in a misleading way. If it was deliberate, they are dishonest. If it was not deliberate, they are incompetent.

The NEA also faults young readers at all three levels for "how poorly" they read, citing the percentages who read below the "proficient" level or the "basic" level, e.g., 36 percent of fourth graders read below the basic level in 2005, and only 31 percent were "proficient" or better. Not mentioned in the report is the fact that there is no empirical basis for determining what score should be considered "basic" or "proficient."

Gerald Bracey has published several penetrating critiques of the NAEP performance levels (see, for example, *Reading Educational Research: How to Avoid Getting Statistically Snookered*) pointing out that the "proficient" level is set very high, and that other countries that consistently rank near the top of the world in reading would not do well on our NAEP: For example, only one-third of Swedish children would be considered "proficient" on the NAEP, nearly the identical percentage of U.S. fourth graders (31 percent in 2005).

The suspicion is that the definition of "proficient" is deliberately set too high, in order to create the illusion that there is, in fact, a crisis in American education, an application of what Naomi Klein has called the "Shock Doctrine," the deliberate creation of a crisis in order to create an environment to institute policies that would be normally unacceptable.

The NEA report itself is, of course, a candidate for an application of the Shock Doctrine, possibly motivated by federal policy on education. Federal policy is based on the assumption that the path to higher literacy is direct instruction in phonics, reading strategies, and vocabulary, not just for the early grades, but for middle school and even higher levels. The problem is that the NEA report contains evidence that another policy, improving access to books, is more appropriate, but avoids embracing it, or even explicitly mentioning it.

"No Single Barrier" to Raising Reading Rates?

The NEA report presents an impressive set of data showing that reading is good for you, that those who read more do better on NAEP tests of reading and writing, and that those with more books in the home do better on NAEP tests of math, science, history, and civics. Having books in the home is, in fact, a better predictor of scores on these tests than is parental education, indicating that it is access to books that is crucial. These findings are consistent with those reported elsewhere (e.g., McQuillan, *The Literacy Crisis: False Claims and Real Solutions,* 1998, and Krashen, *The Power of Reading,* 2004.)

Yet the NEA mysteriously insists that "there is no single barrier, which, if removed, would raise reading rates for young Americans" (p. 41). Of course there is: increasing access to reading materials by improving libraries.

The research is overwhelming. It tells us that those with more access to books read more, and that children of poverty have very little access to books at home, in their communities, or in school (reviewed in Krashen, *The Power of Reading,* 2004). And of course, as noted earlier, the NEA report confirms that more reading leads to better literacy development and more knowledge.

Research done by Keith Curry Lance, Jeff McQuillan, and others also shows that students in schools with higher quality school libraries staffed with credentialed librarians do better on tests of reading, and some of this research specifically shows that library quality (public and school) has a strong relationship with scores on the fourth grade NAEP reading examination: McQuillan (*The Literacy Crisis: False Claims and Real Solutions,* 1998) reported that children in states with better school and public libraries do better on the NAEP, even when the effect of poverty is controlled.

No single factor? How about improving school and public libraries, especially in high poverty areas? The real problem is not a decline but the fact that children of poverty have less access to books and read more poorly than others. This is something we can do something about.

Does Intensive Decoding Instruction Contribute to Reading Comprehension?

6

Originally published in *Knowledge Quest* 37(4): 72–74, 2009.

Summary: *The results of a number of studies point to the conclusion that intensive instruction on decoding helps children do better on tests of decoding, that is, of pronouncing words out loud. Intensive decoding instruction does not make a significant contribution to performance on tests in which children have to understand what they read. These findings suggest that intensive decoding approaches do not lead to real proficiency in literacy.*

In the recent Reading First Impact Final Report, children participating in Reading First classrooms did better than comparisons on a test of decoding given in grade one. Reading First children did not, however, do better on tests of reading comprehension in grades one, two, and three, despite considerable extra instructional time (Gamse et al. 2008).

Not mentioned in the Final Report is that we have seen this pattern before: Children following an intensive, decoding-based curriculum do better on tests of decoding (pronouncing words out loud) when compared to regular students but do not do better on measures of reading comprehension.

Evidence from the National Reading Panel

The pattern of success at decoding and failure at comprehension as a result of intensive phonics instruction was present in the foundation document for Reading First, the report of the National Reading Panel (National Institute of Child Health and Human Development 2000).

The reading panel claimed, on the basis of its review of the research, that intensive systematic phonics was superior to less intensive approaches, but as Garan (2001) has noted, this superiority was present only on tests of decoding, specifically tests on which children pronounce lists of words presented out of context. Children trained with intensive phonics did not do significantly better on tests in which they had to understand what they read: For tests of reading comprehension given after grade one, the impact of intensive systematic phonics was small and statistically insignificant. (For tests given in grades two through six, the effect size on tests of decoding in favor of intensive phonics was substantial: .49 for "decoding regular words" [17 studies], .52 for "decoding irregular words" [13 studies], but only .12 for "comprehending texts" [11 studies].)

Evidence from Direct Instruction

The same pattern is present in research on "Direct Instruction" (DI). Direct Instruction's approach to teaching reading is based on training children in phonemic awareness, followed by drills on phonics. DI maintains that students need to know how to sound out words before they can actually read with understanding.

On "decoding" tests (e.g., the WRAT, Wide Range Achievement Test), DI children do quite well, but their scores are clearly much lower on tests of reading comprehension (e.g., the MAT, Metropolitan Achievement Test, which also includes vocabulary).

This is true when DI children are tested in grade three (Becker et al. 1981) and in grades four, five, and six (summarized in Becker and Gersten 1982, who note that while Direct Instruction children scored at national norms on decoding skills, they only scored between the 25th and 35th percentiles in reading comprehension).

Other follow-up studies show that when DI children are tested in the upper grades on standardized tests that include reading comprehension, the results are extremely modest (grades three, four and five: Meyer, Gersten, and Gutkin 1984; grade nine: Meyer 1984; Gersten, Darch, and Gleason 1988; Gersten, Keating, and Becker 1988; summarized in Adams and Engelmann 1996, p. 94). Ninth-graders in DI scored only at the 34th percentile.

The Clackmannanshire Study

Done in Scotland, the Clackmannanshire study has been cited frequently as a victory for systematic phonics instruction. In first grade (primary 1), two different ways of teaching phonics were compared, and the lessons lasted for 16 weeks. A total of 177 children who received the winning approach, synthetic ("first and fast") phonics, were followed up to grade seven (Johnson and Watson 2005). The comparison group, the one that did not get synthetic phonics but had a different method of learning phonics, was not followed up.

In grade seven, the children were found to be unusually good at pronouncing lists of words presented in isolation, 3.6 years ahead of norms. But they weren't nearly as impressive on tests of reading comprehension, scoring only three months above the expected level.

The children's superior ability to read words out of context did not translate into better reading comprehension ability. In fact, the children were farther above norms in reading comprehension in grade two than in grade seven.

Is Decoding Proficiency Part of Learning to Read?

The results of these studies suggest that a high level of proficiency in decoding is not a preliminary step in learning to read. One could argue, however, that intensive decoding practice is only the first step—necessary, but not sufficient—and it needs to be followed by a great deal of practice in applying the principles learned.

Heavy Skills Instruction Not Necessary

If instruction in decoding is necessary as a first step, the results of other studies indicate that heavy, systematic phonics instruction of the kind supplied by Reading First is not necessary. These studies show that children who have been given the opportunity to do a great deal of interesting, comprehensible reading and have less decoding instruction perform as well as or better than children in decoding-emphasis classes on decoding tests, and typically score higher on tests that test what really counts in reading: comprehension (Morrow, O'Conner, and Smith 1990; Eldridge 1991; Klesius, Griffith, and Zielonka 1991). There are also many attested cases of children who learned to read on their own with little or no explicit decoding instruction and who appear able to decode quite well (e.g., Goodman and Goodman 1982, McQuillan 1998).

In summary: Those who receive only intensive instruction in decoding do not do well on tests of reading comprehension, but those who learn to read by reading, by understanding what is on the page, do well on tests of both decoding and reading comprehension.

Result, Not Cause

This conclusion is consistent with the views of Frank Smith (2004) and Kenneth Goodman (see Flurkey and Xu 2003), who have maintained that our ability to decode complex words is the result of reading, not the cause.

This position does not exclude the teaching of "basic" phonics (Krashen 2004; Garan 2004). A small amount of consciously learned knowledge of the rules of phonics can help in the beginning stages to make texts comprehensible, but there are severe limits on how much phonics can be learned and applied because of the complexity of many of the rules (Smith 2004).

The Reading First Final Report thus confirms the common-sense view that the path to reading proficiency is not through worksheets but through books and stories.

References

Adams, G., and S. Engelmann. 1996. *Research on direct instruction: 25 years beyond DISTAR.* Seattle: Educational Achievement Systems.

Becker, W., S. Englemann, D. Carnine, and R. Rhine. 1981. Direct instruction model. In R. Rhine (Ed.), Making Schools More Effective. New York: Academic Press. pp: 95–154.

Becker, W., and R. Gersten. 1982. Follow-up of follow-through: The later effects of the direct instruction model on children in fifth and sixth grades. *American Educational Research Journal* 19, no. 1 (Spring), 75–92.

Eldridge, L. 1991. An experiment with a modified whole language approach in first-grade classrooms. *Reading Research and Instruction* 30, no. 3, 21–38.

Flurkey, A., and J. Xu, Eds. 2003. *On the revolution in reading: The selected writings of Kenneth S. Goodman.* Portsmouth, NH: Heinemann.

Gamse, B., R. Jacob, M. Horst, B. Boulay, and F. Unlu. 2008. Reading First Impact Study Final Report (NCEE 2009-4038). Washington, DC: National Center for Education Evaluation and Regional Assistance, Institute of Education Sciences, U.S. Department of Education.

Garan, E. 2001. Beyond the smoke and mirrors: A critique of the National Reading Panel report on phonics. *Phi Delta Kappan* 82, no. 7 (March), 500–06.

Garan, E. 2004. *In defense of our children.* Portsmouth: Heinemann.

Gersten, R., T. Keating, and W. Becker. 1988. Continued impact of the Direct Instruction model: Longitudinal studies of Follow Through students. *Education and Treatment of Children* 11: 318–27.

Goodman, K., and Y. Goodman. 1982. Spelling ability of a self-taught reader. In *Language and literacy: The selected writings of Kenneth S. Goodman*, vol. 2., ed. F. Gollasch. London: Routledge, pp. 135–42.

Johnson, R., and J. Watson. 2005. The effects of synthetic phonics teaching on reading and spelling attainment. Scottish Government Publications. http://www.scotland.gov.uk/library5/education/sptrs-00.asp.

Klesius, J., P. Griffith, and P. Zielonkia. 1991. A whole language and traditional instruction comparison: Overall effectiveness and development of the alphabetic principle. *Reading Research and Instruction* 30, 47–61.

Krashen, S. 2004. Basic Phonics. TexTESOL III Newsletter, November 2004, 2–4. Available at www.sdkrashen.com.

McQuillan, J. 1998. Is learning to read without formal instruction common? *Journal of Reading Education* 33, no. 4 (Fall), 15–17.

Meyer, L. 1984. Long-term academic effects of the Direct Instruction project Follow Through. *The Elementary School Journal* 84, no. 4, 380–94.

Meyer, L., R. Gersten, and J. Gutkin. 1983. Direct Instruction: A Project Follow Through success story in an inner-city school. *The Elementary School Journal* 84, no. 2, 241–52.

Morrow, L., E. O'Conner, and J. Smith. 1990. Effects of a story reading program and literacy development of at-risk kindergarten children. *Journal of Reading Behavior* 22, 250–75.

National Institute of Child Health and Human Development. 2000. Report of the National Reading Panel. Teaching children to read: an evidence-based assessment of the scientific research literature on reading and its implications for reading instruction: Reports of the subgroups (NIH Publication No. 00-4754). Washington, DC: U.S. Government Printing Office.

Smith, F. 2004. *Understanding reading*. 6th ed. Hillsdale, NJ: Erlbaum.

Free Voluntary Web-Surfing

7

Originally published in Myers, J., and J. Linzmeier, eds., 2007.
*The Proceedings of 2007 International Conference and Workshop
on TEFL & Applied Linguistics, Department of Applied English,
Ming Chuan University, Taiwan.* Taipei:
Crane Publishing Company, pp. 7–14.

Summary: *This paper presents a simple message: We are taking the wrong approach in our use of computers in language and literacy development. The wrong way is the hard way; the right way is the easy way. "Free voluntary [W]eb-surfing" promises to be a great help for second language acquirers.*

The computer can be used to great advantage in language and literacy development. I present here a view of how this can be done, one that is heavily influenced by the Comprehension Hypothesis—the claim that we acquire language and develop literacy when we understand messages.

The computer can also make things difficult. Approaches that do this assume the correctness of the rival hypothesis, the Skill-Building Hypothesis. Studies of the effectiveness of computer-aided instruction, in fact, typically compare two wrong approaches.

I will first mention some of the problems with current approaches, and then present a much simpler, easier-to-use alternative: free voluntary surfing—doing free voluntary reading on the Internet, or using the Internet to locate printed material of interest for free reading. Free voluntary surfing is rarely mentioned as a possible means of language development. Yet it may have the best potential of all current "computer applications."

The Computer as Skill-Builder

Nearly all applications of the computer to language and literacy development in the early days of computer-aided instruction were based on the Skill-Building Hypothesis, the view that we learn language by first consciously learning about it (learning the rules), being corrected (which helps us "refine" our conscious rules), and practicing the rules until they become "automatic." This tradition continues, despite the overwhelming evidence that skill-building results in very modest amounts of superficial knowledge about language that is difficult to apply to real language use (Krashen 2003).

Inspection of articles published in journals devoted to computer-based instruction (*CALICO* and *ReCALL*; see Zhao 2003 for a review) since their beginning reveals a nearly complete focus on skill-building, and the computer programs involved are generally quite complex. Studies typically deal with the effect of feedback on grammar and pronunciation (Vol. 20, 3, 2000 of *CALICO* is devoted entirely to error correction), various means of presenting and practicing vocabulary and grammar, and comparisons of doing traditional instruction based on skill-building, with and without the computer.

It is no surprise that some studies show that computer-aided approaches are better than non-computer approaches, or that some kinds of computer-aided instruction work better than others, but when both conditions of a study involve skill-building, if skill-building is not the fundamental means by which we acquire language, the information is only of peripheral value.

There is also indirect evidence that this approach has not been useful, i.e., reports that money in schools invested in books is better spent in terms of achievement than money invested in technology (Krashen 1995; Hurd, Dixon, and Olkham 2005).

The Computer as a Source of Written Comprehensible Input

The Comprehension Hypothesis

The Comprehension Hypothesis claims that the processes of comprehension and acquisition are closely related. Comprehension occurs when we make predictions about what we are going to read (or hear) and then attend to enough of the text to confirm that our predictions are correct. Good readers do not examine all details of the text, just enough to have confidence that their predictions are right (Smith 2004; Goodman, in Flurkey and Xu 2003).

For acquisition to occur, the comprehended text needs to contain aspects of language that the acquirer has not yet acquired but is developmentally "ready" to acquire ("i + 1"). I have hypothesized that given enough input, i + 1 is present automatically. We do not need to program texts to make sure the appropriate structures or vocabulary are present, nor is this a good idea (Krashen 1985). When a prediction regarding a previously unknown vocabulary item is successful, we acquire some of the meaning of the word, and as we read and understand the word in subsequent contexts, we gradually build up the full meaning of the word and its grammatical properties.

Our predictions are based on our knowledge of the world, our knowledge of the language, and, in reading, our knowledge of the writing system. This view thus claims that more competence in any of these three sources will increase comprehension by making readers' predictions more accurate, and will thereby increase language acquisition. It also predicts that "easy" texts—texts that contain a high percentage of known language and that are about content familiar to the reader (but with enough new information to stimulate interest)—are optimal for language and literacy development because readers can make better predictions. This prediction is consistent with research showing that that optimal vocabulary development takes place when 95 percent or more of the vocabulary in a text is familiar (Laufer 1992).

In summary: We acquire when we understand what we read or hear; we understand by confirming our predictions about the input and when the input contains new aspects of language we are "ready" to acquire. Acquisition happens gradually and occurs best when texts are very comprehensible.

Acquisition via comprehensible input also happens subconsciously: We are not aware that it is happening while it is happening, and the competence developed this way is stored in the brain subconsciously.

For acquisition to take place optimally, the acquirer also needs to be "open" to the input: High anxiety, low self-esteem, and lack of motivation can lead to a high "affective filter," in which the acquirer may understand the input, but it does not enter "the language acquisition device."

In previous publications, I have also hypothesized that input needs to be interesting for acquisition to take place optimally; high interest ensures that the acquirer will actually pay attention to the input. I now suspect that "interesting" is not enough: The input has be compelling, so interesting that all attention is focused on the message, and thoughts of anxiety do not even occur, so interesting that the acquirer "forgets" that the input is in another language.

A profound difference between the Comprehension Hypothesis and the Skill-Building Hypothesis is that in the former, acquisition of aspects of language such as vocabulary and grammar are the result of acquisition, of receiving comprehensible input. For skill-building, mastery of these aspects needs to precede language acquisition: We first "learn" grammar and vocabulary, then (someday) we can actually use them in comprehension and production. In this sense, the skill-building hypothesis is a delayed gratification hypothesis.

The Power of (Free Voluntary) Reading

There is a great deal of research showing that reading is an excellent source of comprehensible input, and the kind of reading that appears to help the most is the kind most consistent with the principles outlined above: reading that is easily comprehensible and compelling, reading that the reader selects, also known as "free voluntary reading" (Krashen 2004), reading that is done with no "accountability," no testing, no book reports, but for its own sake, for pleasure.

The Computer as a Source of Comprehensible Texts

There have been some attempts to use the computer and the Internet to supply comprehensible input. (I will not discuss aural comprehensible input here, but invite the reader to visit eslpod.com, which is an excellent source of interesting aural English input for second language acquirers.)

The Internet offers many simplified texts in English. Only a small minority, however, have the potential of being genuinely interesting. But even when the texts are reasonable, they are often followed by a long parade of comprehension questions and exercises.

Of course, the Internet also supplies authentic texts in English, and the selection is enormous. Nearly every acquirer can find something of interest. The question is how to make these texts comprehensible for second language acquirers.

Before proceeding, we need to discuss one more aspect of the comprehension hypothesis and how it is applied: narrow reading.

The Comprehension Hypothesis predicts that self-selected narrow reading is optimal for language and literacy development. As described elsewhere (Krashen 1981, 2004), narrow reading means focusing on one topic, author, or genre, according to the reader's interests, and gradually expanding the range of what is read over time. It is the opposite of the "survey" approach.

Self-selection and narrow reading nearly guarantee interest and comprehensibility because of greater background knowledge, which increases as readers read more, and because of greater knowledge of the language: Each writer has favorite expressions and a distinctive style, and each topic has its own vocabulary and discourse. Thus narrow reading results in rapid acquisition of the "language" of the author or topic, and provides built-in review.

The evidence in favor of narrow reading is of two kinds. First, there is overwhelming evidence supporting free voluntary reading in general, evidence from case histories, correlational studies, and studies of in-school sustained silent reading (Krashen 2004). Also, studies specifically show that those who do narrow reading make excellent progress (Cho and Krashen 1994, 1995a, 1995b), that better readers are typically narrow readers (Lamme 1976), and that a substantial percentage of books that children enjoy are "series" books of some kind (Ujiie and Krashen 2002, 2005).

It also appears to be the case that narrow readers gradually expand their reading interests (LaBrant, 1958); we need not fear that narrow readers will stay with one kind of reading forever.

Also, narrow reading does not result in the ability to read in only one area. Deep reading in any topic will provide exposure to a tremendous amount of syntax and vocabulary that is used in other topics.

Reading instruction for those beyond the initial stages, according to the Comprehension Hypothesis, is focused on helping readers find appropriate texts, and encouraging narrow reading.

Free Voluntary Surfing

The best use of the computer, given today's technology, may be the most straightforward: Free Voluntary Surfing (FVS), simply encouraging English as a foreign language (EFL) students to wander through the Internet and read what interests them, following their interests from site to site, and from site to print.

In this section, I present some evidence that FVS can, in fact, result in higher levels of literacy, and that many EFL students already possess the necessary competence to do it, but do not. I then consider what might be holding them back and what we can do about it.

FVS and Language/Literacy Development

Evidence for the potential of the Internet in EFL comes from Cho and Kim (2004), who reported that children in EFL classes in Korea that included reading interesting stories of their choice from the Internet gained significantly more in English than comparisons did. This was not, however, genuine "surfing." The children read from selected Web sites, and the duration of the study was only 14 weeks, so the full potential of surfing was not realized.

Jackson et al. (2006) provided computers with Internet access to 140 children (ages 10–18, but mostly between 12–14) from low-income families. Jackson et al. reported that more Internet use resulted in improved reading, as reflected by grades and standardized tests. The improvements were present after six months of Internet use for test scores and after one year for grades. There was no impact on mathematics test scores, and the data did not support the hypothesis that better readers used the Internet more; rather, Internet use improved reading.

Jackson et al. (2006) point out that "[W]eb pages are heavily text based" (p. 433), and suggest that it was self-motivated reading of these texts that was the cause of the gains in reading. de Haan and Huysmans (2004) reported, however, that for adolescents in the Netherlands, greater use of the Internet is modestly positively correlated with use of print media (r = .31): those who used the Internet more also read regular print more. In addition, Lee and Kuo (2002) reported that an increase in use of the Internet over a one-year period was associated with more newspaper reading (and less television) for secondary school students in Singapore: During this time, Internet use increased from 73 percent to 87 percent of the sample (n = 817). A similar result has been reported for adults in Taiwan (Liu, Day, Sun, and Wany 2000).

Of course it is possible that this result is influenced by social class: More affluent people have more access to both computers and books. Despite this lack of control, it is possible that Internet use does indeed lead to more reading via the computer, which in turn may be responsible for growth in reading.

Jackson et al. (2006) reported no relationship between non-Internet use of the computer and amount of use of printed media ($r = -.04$); the positive relationship held only for the use of the Internet. For adults in the United States, however, more computer use in general is associated with time spent reading, even when controlled for social class. The relationship, though, is modest (Robinson and Godbey 1997).

A logical study would be to determine the existence of the relationships (regression coefficients) in the model presented in figure 1, controlling for poverty. Both reading from the Internet and free voluntary reading stimulated by Internet use may be directly related to reading achievement, or the effect of Internet use might be indirect, with only reading print media directly relating to reading achievement. (In the case of the low-income children studied in Jackson et al. 2006, however, it is doubtful that they had much access to print media; see Neuman and Celano 2001.)

Figure 1 Hypothesized relationships among Internet use, free reading (use of print media), and reading achievement

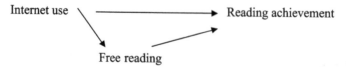

An obvious gap in the research, as Jackson and colleagues note, is that only "time on the [I]nternet" was considered as a predictor, with no attempt made to determine the impact of different kinds of Internet use (e.g., blogs, reading the news, games, etc.). Nevertheless, the results of Jackson et al. (2006) are consistent with the Comprehension Hypothesis.

The Popularity of the Internet and Web-Surfing

It has been widely reported that Internet use is increasing in many countries, and that a significant number of people use the Internet for free voluntary Web-surfing. Horrigan (2006) reported a tremendous increase in Internet use in the United States, with estimated growth from 60 million in March 2005 (30 percent of all adults) to 84 million one year later, in March 2006 (42 percent of the adult population).

Two-thirds of Internet users admit that they engage in free voluntary surfing "at some time." Fallows (2006) concluded that "surfing for fun" is the second most popular online activity, behind using e-mail. Similarly, Zhu and He (2002) reported that 52 percent of the 1007 Hong Kong residents they interviewed were connected to the Internet at home, averaging 350 minutes per week on the Net at home (and another 629 minutes at work). Interviewees said they spent an average of 104 minutes "searching for personal [I]nternet information," about 30 percent of the total home-use time.

The children included the Michigan State study clearly liked Web-surfing: When asked what their main activity on the computer was, 33 percent said it was "[W]eb search" (Jackson, von Eye, Biocca, Barbatsis, Zhao, and Fitzgerald 2005, p. 263).

A Reluctance to Surf in EFL?

A survey done in adults (over age 18) in Taiwan in 2000 (Liu, Day, Sun, and Wany 2000) reported that about 25 percent of those interviewed (488/2015) were Internet users. Most of this use, however, was on Chinese-language Web sites, with 84 percent of users' time on Taiwanese Web sites and about 6 percent on overseas Chinese Web sites. Liu et al. cite a previous survey done by Yams (a search engine used in Taiwan) that found similar results. According to the Yams study, about 70 percent of the time spent on Web sites using other languages was with English language Web sites, and about 7 percent with Japanese language Web sites. We can thus estimate that only 7 percent of users' time on the Internet involves English.

Of those using English Web sites, however, some are undoubtedly those with very high proficiency in English already. These results suggest that few people take advantage of the Internet as a source of input in English as a second or foreign language.

In addition, use of FVS for helping language development is rarely mentioned in articles devoted to pedagogy; when the Internet is mentioned at all, the discussion is usually about how helping students learn to use the computer—the target population we are talking about is already comfortable surfing the Web in their first language—or finding specific information on the Internet as specified by the teacher (see, e.g., articles in the "Internet" section of http://iteslj.org/Lessons/).

I suspect that the reasons for the lack of use of FVS are similar to the reasons why free voluntary reading is underused. Instructors and those creating materials may be hesitant to include it because of a belief in the Skill-Building Hypothesis, the importance of knowing every word in a text, and a lack of faith in language acquisition. Another factor could be the fear that EFL Web-surfers will stick with easy, familiar reading and never progress to harder material that will help them make progress. As noted above, this is not the case in print reading, but this possibility should be investigated.

The most obvious reason EFL students do not try FVS is that it is never mentioned in class, which is also the case for FVR. Thus, most students have developed the same personal theories about language acquisition and literacy development that the curriculum reflects, i.e., the Skill-Building Hypothesis. They have little choice: In general, no alternative is presented to them.

EFL students may also fear that authentic texts will be incomprehensible, unaware that narrow reading on familiar and compelling topics, without knowing every word, will contribute to making these texts comprehensible and thereby contribute to language acquisition.

The best way, in my experience, to get a feel for narrow FVS is to try it. The Internet provides a unique opportunity to test the effects of narrow reading on oneself without expending a lot of effort in finding relevant and related reading material.

Let me suggest the following guidelines:

1.   Do FVS in a language you are "intermediate" in, one in which you can read some authentic texts.

2.   Start FVS by looking at Google News, or Web sites on any topic you are interested in. It is, I think, crucial not to choose a topic that is professionally relevant, or even important to your life. If the reading is "serious," you may revert to intensive word-perfect reading. Choose something genuinely interesting but not essential: In other words, don't use FVS, at least at first, to make you a better person.

3.   Accept the fact that it will take you a while to find a topic and that it will take you a while to overcome the habit of not looking up words. The two problems will probably be solved at the same time: When you find an area that is really compelling, you will not be tempted to look up words. In fact, you will barely be aware that you are reading in another language. And that is when real language acquisition takes place (see chapter eight, this volume).

Conclusion

We should at least consider the most obvious, least expensive, and least complex application of the computer to language education, especially with those students who have already mastered the technical aspects of Internet use. All we need to do is to encourage them to do something they already enjoy doing in their first language.

References

Cho, K. S., and Hee-Jung Kim. 2004. Recreational reading in English as a foreign language in Korea: Positive effects of a sixteen-week program. *Knowledge Quest* 32(4): 47–49.

Cho, K. S., and S. Krashen. 1994. Acquisition of vocabulary from the Sweet Valley High Kids series: Adult ESL acquisition. *Journal of Reading* 37: 662–67.

Cho, K. S., and S. Krashen. 1995a. From Sweet Valley Kids to Harlequins in one year. *California English,* 1(1): 18–19.

Cho, K. S., and S. Krashen. 1995b. Becoming a dragon: Progress in English as a second language through narrow free voluntary reading. *California Reader* 29: 9–10.

de Haan, J., and F. Huysmans. 2004. IT/Media use and psychological development among Dutch youth. *IT&Society* 1(7): 44–58.

Fallows, D. 2006. Pew Internet Project Data Memo, February 2006.

Flurkey, A., and J. Xu, eds. 2003. *On the revolution in reading: The selected writings of Kenneth S. Goodman.* Portsmouth, NH: Heinemann.

Horrigan, J. 2006. *Home broadband adoption.* Pew Report, May 28, 2006.

Hurd, S., M. Dixon, and J. Olkham. 2005. Are low levels of book spending in primary schools jeopardizing the National Literacy Strategy? *The Curriculum Journal* 17(1): 73–88

Jackson, L., A. Von Eye, F. Biocca, G. Barbatsis, Y. Zhao, and H. Fitzgerald. 2005. How low-income children use the Internet at home. *Journal of Interactive Learning Research* 16(3): 259–72.

Jackson, L., A. Von Eye, F. Biocca, G. Barbatsis, Y. Zhao, and H. Fitzgerald. 2006. Does home Internet use influence the academic performance of low-income children? *Developmental Psychology* 42(3): 429–33.

Krashen, S. 1981. The case for narrow reading. *TESOL Newsletter* 15: 23.

Krashen, S. 1985. *The input hypothesis.* New York: Longman.

Krashen, S. 1995. School libraries, public libraries, and the NAEP reading scores. *School Library Media Quarterly* 23: 235–38.

Krashen, S. 2003. *Explorations in language acquisition and use: The Taipei lectures.* Portsmouth, NH: Heinemann. Also available through Crane Publishing Company, Taipei, Taiwan.

Krashen, S. (2004). *The power of reading.* Portsmouth, NH: Heinemann, and Westport, CT: Libraries Unlimited.

LaBrant, L. 1958. *An evaluation of free reading.* In *Research in the three R's,* ed. C. Hunnicutt and W. Iverson. New York: Harper and Brothers, pp. 154–61.

Lamme, L. 1976. Are reading habits and abilities related? *Reading Teacher* 30: 21–27.

Laufer, B. 1992. How much lexis is necessary for reading comprehension? In *Vocabulary and applied linguistics,* ed. P. J. Arnaud and H. Béjoint. London: Macmillan, pp. 126–32.

Lee, W., and E. Kuo. 2002. Internet and displacement effect: Media use and activities in Singapore. *Journal of Computer-Mediated Communication,* January 7(2).

Liu, C-C, W-W Day, S-W Sun, and G. Wang. 2002. User behavior and the "globalness" of the Internet: From a Taiwan users' perspective. *Journal of Computer-Mediated Communication,* January 7(2).

Neuman, S., and D. Celano. 2001. Access to print in low-income and middle-income communities. *Reading Research Quarterly* 36(1), 8–26.

Robinson, J., and G. Godbey. 1997. *Time for life: The surprising way Americans use their time.* University Park, PA: University of Pennsylvania Press.

Smith, F. 2004. *Understanding reading.* 6th ed. Hillsdale, NJ: Erlbaum.

Ujiie, J., and S. Krashen. 2002. Home run books and reading enjoyment, *Knowledge Quest* 31(1): 36–37.

Ujiie, J., and S. Krashen. 2005. Are prize-winning books popular among children? An analysis of public library circulation. *Knowledge Quest* 34 (3): 33–35.

Zhao, Y. 2003. Recent developments in technology and language learning: A literature review and meta-analysis. *CALICO Journal*, 21(1): 7–21.

Zhu, J., and Z. He. 2002. Diffusion, use and impact of the Internet in Hong Kong: A chain process model. *Journal of Computer-Mediated Communication*, January 7(2).

Hypotheses About Free Voluntary Reading

8

Originally published in Myers, J., and J. Linzmeier, eds. *The Proceedings of 2007 International Conference and Workshop on TEFL & Applied Linguistics, Department of Applied English, Ming Chuan University*, Taiwan. Taipei: Crane Publishing Company, pp. 656–58.

Summary: *I present here four hypotheses that deepen previous hypotheses about language acquisition and literacy development: (1) Language acquisition occurs most efficiently when we are so involved in the message that we "forget" it is in another language, or that it contains aspects of language that we have not yet acquired. (2) For reading to best stimulate language development, it should appear to be effortless. (3) Readers acquire best when they are not aware that they are improving. They are only aware of the content of what they have read. (4) The more we check comprehension, the less readers understand and the less they acquire.*

I am not claiming that the following hypotheses are true. They are, after all, hypotheses. Thus far, they are supported by the evidence, and there is no counterevidence. Research directed at finding supporting evidence or evidence contrary to these hypotheses will advance the field. This means that they are "good" hypotheses, right or wrong.

These hypotheses assume the correctness of: the Acquisition-Learning, Natural Order, Monitor, Comprehension (including the Reading Hypothesis), and Affective Filter hypotheses, for both aural and written language, first and second language, and acquirers of all ages (Krashen 2003, 2004).

The Forgetting Hypothesis

Language acquisition occurs most efficiently when we are so inter-ested in the message that we "forget" that it contains new grammar and vocabulary, or, in the case of second language readers, that it is in another language. This hypothesis is consistent with earlier hypotheses: The Comprehension Hypothesis requires that input be comprehensible, and the affective filter hypothesis requires that anxiety be low. The Forgetting Hypothesis requires that the message be not only comprehensible and interesting but compelling, which focuses all attention on the message so that thoughts of anxiety do not even occur.

The Forgetting Hypothesis is influenced by the concept of "flow" (Csikszentmihalyi 1993). Flow is the state people reach when they are deeply but effortlessly involved in an activity. In flow, the concerns of everyday life and even the sense of self disappear—our sense of time is altered, and nothing but the activity itself seems to matter. "Forgetting" and flow occur in reading when readers are "lost in a book," when they are aware only of the story or the message in the text. It is when this happens that language acquisition occurs most effectively. Note that this position is the opposite of the "focus on form" or "focus on forms" points of view.

The Effortless Reading Hypothesis

The best reading for language development is easy reading, reading that seems to be completely comprehensible without struggle. Effortless Reading may be a prerequisite to "Forgetting": Getting lost in a book is only possible when comprehension is not a barrier. Thus:

Effortless Reading > Forgetting

The Effortless Reading Hypothesis is consistent with Laufer (1992): For optimal vocabulary development, at least 95 percent of the words in a text need to be known, which suggests that optimal acquisition requires a high level of comprehension.

The Unawareness of Acquisition Hypothesis

This hypothesis states that readers will not be aware that they are improving while they are reading, but will only be aware of reading interesting books.

I suspect that those who "forget" they are reading in another language are also unaware that they are acquiring. Thus:

Forgetting > Unawareness of Acquisition, and thus:
Effortless Reading > Forgetting > Unawareness of Acquisition

Evidence for this hypothesis are cases in which acquirers (1) are "surprised" to discover that they had acquired something they didn't know they had acquired and (2) were aware of their competence but didn't know where it came from (e.g., the case of Y. Cohen, discussed in Krashen 2004).

Lin, Shin, and Krashen (2007) present the case of Sophia, a high school student who came to the United States with her family when she was in sixth grade. Her high school reading test scores showed a strange pattern: During the academic year, they declined, but over the summer, they increased. During the summer Sophia would make up the loss of the year, and then some.

The answer to this mystery was that Sophia was a dedicated summer pleasure reader, reading about 50 books during each summer. She had, however, little time for pleasure reading during the academic year. Sophia's reading was not a deliberate strategy for improving her English. She did it for pleasure. The discovery of the pattern of her exam scores occurred later, after she had been a summer reader for several years.

The Comprehension Checking Hypothesis

The more we check comprehension, the less readers understand and the less they acquire. Comprehension checking asks readers to remember what they are reading while they are reading, which means less engagement, less flow, less losing oneself in the text, and, as a consequence, less "forgetting" that they are reading in another language. More comprehension checking also means less enjoyment of reading.

It is predicted that both *more frequent* and *more detailed* comprehension checking are related to less comprehension.

Table 1 presents the kinds of comprehension checking typically done, in reverse order of their predicted level of interference with flow and comprehension. Those closer to the bottom are more likely to have the goal of ensuring that students have actually read the book.

Table 1
Types of Comprehension Checking

1. Nothing required: discussion and writing about what is read is optional
2. Required writing: how the reading is relevant to the reader
3. Summary writing
4. Comprehension questions: high level (gist)
5. Comprehension questions: low level (details)

The presence of comprehension questions can send the message that we do not trust the reader to actually do the reading and that even self-selected reading is unpleasant. Comprehension questions can "turn play into work."

The idea that compulsion is not ideal for learning in general is an old one: "Compulsory physical exercise does no harm to the body, but compulsory learning never sticks in the mind . . ." (Plato, pp. 269–70).

Consistent with this hypothesis is the finding that sustained silent reading, which does not require comprehension checking, typically produces results superior to traditional instruction.

Conclusions

These hypotheses claim that language development happens in small steps beneath the level of awareness, and occurs when the reader's attention is directed not at the language but at a message that the reader (or listener) thinks is very interesting.

They claim that grim determination and struggle are not part of the language development process, that there is no need for the delayed gratification that is core to skill-building. In fact, the hypotheses presented here claim that pain and struggle indicate that language acquisition is not taking place (although conscious language learning might be).

They also maintain that the path of language and literacy development, while obeying universal principles of language acquisition, is individual, in the sense that different people have different interests and backgrounds. A text that results in flow in one reader will not necessarily have this effect in other readers.

References

Csikszentmihalyi, M. 1992. *Flow: The psychology of optimal experience.* New York: HarperPerennial.

Krashen, S. 2004. *The power of reading.* 2nd ed. Portsmouth, NH: Heinemann, and Westport, CT: Libraries Unlimited.

Laufer, B. 1992. How much lexis is necessary for reading comprehension? In *Vocabulary and applied linguistics,* ed. P. J. Arnaud and H. Béjoint. London: Macmillan, pp. 126–32.

Lin, S-Y, F. Shin, and S. Krashen. 2007. Sophia's choice: Summer reading. *Knowledge Quest* 35 (4).

Plato. *The republic.* 2nd ed. Translated by Desmond Lee. London: Penguin. Part VIII, book 7, pp. 269–70.

Index

Accelerated Reader, 46, 47, 48, 49, 50 (cost of)
access (to books), 6, 7, 35, 38, 39, 47, 59
accountability, 10
Achterman, D., 7, 10
affective filter, 70
Anderson, R., 5, 10, 24, 31
Appleby, B., 8, 10
Aranha, M., 40
Atwell, N., 49, 51

Becker, W., 62, 63, 65
Bell, T., 34, 37, 41
Bible reading, 5, 12
Book displays, 8
Bracey, G., 58
Brassell, D., 7, 11

Calkins, H., 2, 11
Celano, D. 7, 17, 74, 79
Cho, G., 3, 19, 25, 29
Cho, K.S., 2, 3, 5, 7, 9, 11, 41, 72, 73, 78
Choi, D.S., 7, 11
Clackmannanshire Study, 63
Cloze tests, 33, 34
Cohen, J., 48, 51
Cohen, K., 4, 12
Comics, 8, 9, 25

compelling input, 70, 71, 77, 82
Comprehension checking, 40
Comprehension Checking Hypothesis, 83
Comprehension Hypothesis, 28, 65, 69, 70, 71, 72, 74, 81
Constantino, R., 5, 7, 12, 19
Csikszentmihalyi, M., 82, 85
Cultural literacy, 5, 20
Cunningham, A., 8, 19

Day, R., 2, 13, 27, 30
decline in reading, 9, 53, 54
decoding, 61, 62, 63
dementia, 6
direct instruction, 62
de Haan, J., 73, 78
Dupuy, B., 3, 20
Duke, N., 7, 20

eating and reading, 10
Effortless Reading Hypothesis, 82
Eldridge, L., 64, 65
Elley, W., 2, 12, 29, 41
Entwhistle, J., 4, 20
eslpod.com, 71
Evans, M., 7, 12

Fallows, D., 75, 78
Farmer, L., 50, 52

About the Author

DR. STEPHEN KRASHEN is an advocate for free voluntary reading in schools. He also closely follows media coverage of local, state, and national activities that reflect on student learning. He responds with letters to the editors of journals and newspapers across the country, defending the rights of children to read, describing the need for access to school and public libraries, and the benefits of having professionally trained and certified school librarians to support student reading.

About the Author

Lightning Source UK Ltd.
Milton Keynes UK
UKHW02f2357180918
329095UK00004B/222/P